# Poetry in Motion

# From Coast To Coast
Edited by Donna Samworth

E. Doubleday.
18/5/2004.

 Young**Writers**

First published in Great Britain in 2004 by:
Young Writers
Remus House
Coltsfoot Drive
Peterborough
PE2 9JX
Telephone: 01733 890066
Website: www.youngwriters.co.uk

SB ISBN 1 84460 406 3

# Foreword

This year, the Young Writers' 'Poetry In Motion' competition proudly presents a showcase of the best poetic talent selected from over 40,000 up-and-coming writers nationwide.

Young Writers was established in 1991 to promote the reading and writing of poetry within schools and to the youth of today. Our books nurture and inspire confidence in the ability of young writers and provide a snapshot of poems written in schools and at home by budding poets of the future.

The thought effort, imagination and hard work put into each poem impressed us all and the task of selecting poems was a difficult but nevertheless enjoyable experience.

We hope you are as pleased as we are with the final selection and that you and your family continue to be entertained with *Poetry In Motion From Coast To Coast* for many years to come.

# Contents

Luke Wassell  (12)                                  121
Joshua Coles  (12)                                  122
Kelly-Marie Tuck  (15)                              123
Catherine Barlett  (12)                             124
Justin Klausner  (13)                               125
Laura Black  (12)                                   126
Victoria Leggett  (15)                              127
Kayleigh Jane Bartram  (15)                         128
Abdul Hamza-Aly  (13)                               129
Callum Connell  (12)                                130
Andrew Allcock  (13)                                131
Jack Denny  (12)                                    132
Sam Bernthal  (13)                                  133
Lewis Tyler  (13)                                   134
Christopher Smith  (12)                             135
Lakhdar Merahi  (13)                                136
Cloe Peters  (14)                                   137
Peter Armfield  (14)                                138
Duncan Boyne  (12)                                  139
Saskia Cook  (12)                                   140
Adam Frosdick  (12)                                 141
Adam Fairhead  (13)                                 142
Samantha Bishop  (12)                               143
Chloe Simmons  (13)                                 144
Jordan Lee  (14)                                    145
Simone Garland  (13)                                146
Keomi Farnsworth  (12)                              147
Connel Hooley  (13)                                 148
Luke Prettyman  (15)                                149
Adam Cairney  (13)                                  150

## Greenfield School Community & Art College, Newton Aycliffe
Phillippa Pearson  (12)                             151
Abbie Sowerby  (11)                                 152
Emma Peart  (11)                                    153
Charlotte Howells  (11)                             154
Natasha Griffin  (12)                               155
Megan Davies-Brown  (11)                            156
Matthew Linsley  (11)                               157
Martin Clarke  (12)                                 158
Benita MacDonald  (11)                              159

## St Leonard's RC Comprehensive School, Durham

| | |
|---|---|
| Michael Robson (14) | 199 |
| Matthew James Turnbull (15) | 200 |
| Katie McElroy (15) | 201 |
| Amy Spence (14) | 202 |
| Sarah Clough (14) | 203 |
| Robert Miles (14) | 204 |
| Ben Jones (14) | 205 |
| Maria Smith (15) | 206 |

## Sheringham Woodfields (Special) School, Sheringham

| | |
|---|---|
| Steven Wright (13) | 207 |
| Andrew Easton (11) | 208 |
| Frank Butt (13) | 209 |
| Danny Bridges (13) | 210 |

# The Poems

# Anger

It's building up inside of you
waiting to come out.
A tension pushing out of you
that makes you want to shout!

You want to scream
and kick and shout
and break and shake
and run about!

You want to squeeze
so terribly tight
and pinch something
with all your might.

You want to do something
horribly mean
that makes you let out a
gigantic *scream!*

**Jessica Brown  (12)**

# Teams

Teams are like a bale of hay,
Stick together,
Never parting,
Only split by ending of life.
String together in what they do,
Succeeding.
Though splitting in troubled times,
Always,
Again rejoining.

Each member important
As another.
Dying if one leaves,
Forever ending.

**Matt Jewell  (11)**

# The Summer Hols

It's coming near,
it's something to fear,
six weeks alone
sitting at home
with no mates
and no dates!

You have to find a job,
maybe walk a dog?
Six weeks alone,
sitting at home
with just Mum and Dad
trying not to be bad!

Summer hols, good for some,
go abroad and sit in the sun,
six weeks alone
sitting at home
waiting for a card
that says 'You retard'!

I'm glad that's not me
I'm not going to be . . .
six weeks alone
sitting at home
with no mates
and no dates!

**Amber Savins  (13)**

# Teams

*(This poem is about the Portuguese fishermen in the town of Burgow in the Algarve)*

They get up early in the morning,
And push their boats out when the sun is dawning.
They go out in twos, rowing out to sea,
Hoping to catch eels, dorado or bree,
They throw their nets out hoping to catch,
Like the British army's royal despatch.
When the sun's right up they head for home,
With their morning catch after the morning's sea roam.
They pull their boats up on the beach,
Bring the fish in their net like breach.
They empty their nets and light the barbecue,
And then cook the fish and make a lovely stew.
They then sell it to the restaurants along the beach,
Then they all dream about that catch which was so hard to reach.

**Lewis Holden**

# The Book Of Life

I often sit up in my room,
Upon my silver chair.
I stumble upon the Book of Life,
And guess what I find there . . . ?

A babbling brook,
Weaving its way in the countryside.
I follow its path and lose myself,
As I prepare for a lengthy ride.

The source is slow and calm,
Tumbling gently along.
The river soon quickens the pace,
And I can't help but sing my song.

The water is so fast and furious,
As I'm thrown to and fro.
And whilst I hold on to my seat,
I feel the flowing slow.

The end is creeping into sight,
I'm feeling rather weary.
I feel my eyelids flutter shut,
And leave this world quite teary.

So as I sit up in my room,
Upon my silver chair,
I close for now the Book of Life,
And relive what I found there.

**Clare Williams  (13)**

# First Impressions

My first impression
Was the size of the school!
Compared to middle school
It was as big as a museum,
The noise like a herd of stampeding elephants.

I thought I
Would get lost
But I did not
I was scared
Of getting lost.

The dinners
Had a wide
Selection of food
There were chips, crisps
And burgers.

I was frightened
In case I got
Bullied or people
Called me names
But I did not get bullied.

I was scared
In case the teachers
Were nasty but they
Were not, they were kind
They helped me when I was stuck.

**Aaron Paul Gallagher  (13)**
**Astley High School, Seaton Delaval**

# Backfire

There was a young gent called Dob,
Who was a massive big snob,
His best mate was named Dennis,
Who was a true menace,
He tricked Dob one day,
By saying his name was Fay,
It backfired on him,
When Dob told Tim,
Tim bought him a frock,
And his mom sent him to an insane dock!

**Stephen Stanners  (13)**
**Astley High School, Seaton Delaval**

# Just Pure Stupid

Things to do before I die . . .

First, I'm going to fly
Second I will fall into a mall
Third I will find my cheese

Things that are useful to know . . .

Bees will pay my fees
Once I've done that I will eat some peas
So I can go home with ease
And then at least fleas won't tease

The thing that is wrong with me . . .

I had a sore toe that I once saw
It had turned suddenly into a paw
Oh I wish I would talk
But not without my cork
Because then I could not stalk
That dog with my pork.

**Matthew Warner  (13)**
**Astley High School, Seaton Delaval**

# Skin Collar

Sickness spreading everywhere
Sickness creeps inside
Sickness feeds off everything
Sickness grows in time

Darkness is reflecting us
Darkness of all kinds
Darkness always choosing us
Darkness rules our lives

You can fight
You can sit back
Life's a suitcase
That you've got to pack.

**Rosanna Hoar  (15)**
**Astley High School, Seaton Delaval**

# Lost Love

I often sit and wonder,
Where did the world go by?
I usually come to the conclusion,
It must have just slipped by,
Some day when I was busy,
Or even with nothing to do,
I think it may have been better,
Had I spent more time with you.

The few precious moments we had together,
Will always be deep in my heart.
I couldn't hide my emotions,
When we were made to part.
I never will forget you,
No matter how hard I try,
I wouldn't want to anyway,
Not until the day I die.

**Deborah Graham (15)**
**Astley High School, Seaton Delaval**

# The Cycle

The bottle clinks against his teeth,
making a slight chink.
The bottle, empty, not a glass but still,
he throws it in the sink.
The bottle clatters, glass shatters,
still he walks away.
He opens the fridge and takes another,
this is the eighth today.
His wife walks in and sees his sin,
sadly she shakes her head.
She walks upstairs, leaves well alone,
he might as well be dead.
From the bottle he sucks and sucks,
but really it sucks from him.
It works and works on his body,
giving him yellow skin.
His son sees what's going on,
but can he change his fate?
Break the cycle, get out of the net,
turn into something great?
Only time will tell what will happen,
with enough time and space.
Break the spell, get out of the net.
End the never-ending race!

**Kimberley Smith  (15)**
**Astley High School, Seaton Delaval**

# Cancer

Cancer is . . .

Cancer is tearing me apart.
Cancer is breaking my heart.
Cancer is in my head.
Cancer is under my bed.
Cancer is burning away.
Cancer, I hope, isn't going to stay.
I pray to God, *'Please let it go away.'*
But I know things will be OK.
I love you, Dad.

**Jennifer McLaughlin (14)**
**Astley High School, Seaton Delaval**

# My First Words Of My Life

My first impressions of my life were when my brother said to me,
'When you go to school, always listen to the teacher.'

My brother is so useless,
my brother never listens,
but when he tells me to listen, I never understand,
but I go to my mum and say, 'Mum, he never listens.'
And then my mum says, 'Always listen,'
but I still don't understand.
*Then* I go to my dad and say, 'Dad, Mum and Bill are going mad
by saying, 'Always listen.'
'Well, they might be right about it because you will never learn
how to understand what the teacher or anyone else is saying.'
'OK, Dad, I understand.'
The first day I went to school and the teacher was saying something
about maths and he said, 'Does anyone know the answer?'
I put my hand up and said, '100, Sir.'

The moral of the poem is always listen because you will never get
anywhere in life, especially when it comes to listening to a policeman
or someone like him.

When you listen you will be able to get anything you want in life.

**Lewis Dry  (13)**
**Astley High School, Seaton Delaval**

# Hallowe'en

Trick or treat,
Hallowe'en's funny I think,
because nobody knows what they seem to be,
there are ghouls and ghosts and zombie hosts,
and lots of yummy candy.
Children shout out loud and clear,
they chill my spine and hurt my ear.
The moon comes up, the sun goes down,
while ghouly friends come from the ground.
Now goodnight children,
hop it quick,
cos ugly monsters will make you sick.

*Trick or treat,* Hallowe'en's funny . . . I think.

**Shannen Riches  (12)**
**Cliff Park High School, Gorleston**

# The Arranged Marriage

The disillusioned bride felt a threat,
That one day her loneliness would have to go.
Her parents would disregard her cretinous belief
And surely her smile would cover all?

Her hair so flowing, would stop abruptly,
And in her mind she toyed with the idea of having a Medusa head,
But soon her smiles would fade away.
To be told who, and when, and 'Oh, you must!'
Made her pure Madonna-skin seem as rough as a furrowed field.

Her eyes, so colourless but holding so much emotion,
Her magazines filled with fantasies - from the hunk of the month
To the problem pages.
She wouldn't let her parents control, determine or dictate her future!
A slight pain at the brow, and a piercing piece of a dream
She once had in her toddler days.
A voice calmly reminding her to take the forward, left path or right,
But never down the aisle!
Wow, her 20/20 wedding vision was still sharp!

**Mercedes Bailey (12)**
**Cliff Park High School, Gorleston**

# Visions

It was smooth,
The vision of the animal came back to me,
It was violent,
Some visions like death before me.
I knew this must be a mission,
Or I guessed anyway.
I think.
*This is going to get grotesque.*
The mission can now commence,
Let's go,
Delve into my vision and see my experiences.

**Jennifer Folkes-Allen (12)**
**Cliff Park High School, Gorleston**

# Winter

Perfectly dressed trees covered in a party of green leaves,
About to be victims of winter's deadly wrath,
Unable to defend, mindlessly winter dresses them into grotesque
brown cloaks,
Sorrow falls upon them as they drift down and die.

**Amy Colella  (12)**
**Cliff Park High School, Gorleston**

# Jewellery

A thousand riches for the entire world to see
Their splendour and elegance,
Scattered bones upon the floor,
Littered with remains of forgotten dreams.

From years past, each memory
Tightly sealed within the locket.
Love's first embrace kept hidden away,
Preserved so well, yet the face now a ghost
As time dragged on, with no tune or song.

Pearls now dull from times so enchanting,
Like the faces worn now,
Tired and grey.
No second thoughts given to naïve young youth,
Life's now so important,
Memories left alone, true feelings forgotten.

Dreaming and dancing, shut into the past,
No fun or amusement,
Life now a task.
People so happy
Painted smiles to pretend,
No talking, just hush, the silence, a friend.

Lost friendships, lost laughter, no time for the past
People just living
Hidden tight behind the mask.

As the chill sets in
Wrapping heart and soul,
Freezing the mind, thoughts on hold,
The thousand riches
Now taken by the sea
Yet the wounds still open,
Jagged emotions cutting free.

Memories tucked away
The mind's pocket now full
Treasured so secretly
Hidden with bright eyes, and
A painted smile
To pretend.

**Shaffia Khan (16)**
**Cliff Park High School, Gorleston**

# My Lover, My Friend

A friend who knows my deepest secrets
A lover who I see and instantly get shivers
A friend who needs a friend
A lover who needs to be loved
A heart that's yet to be broken
Feelings that are yet to be spoken
A love without a cure
No uncertainties for sure

Such a shame how I mesmerise
Caught a glimpse of Heaven looking in his eyes
Feels like snow caressing mountain tops
I've found love's treasure in this ocean of pleasure
Because his kisses make my lips quiver
And when he touches me my whole body shivers
When the world starts to stress me out
Where I run is to his arms, without a doubt
He's like a drug, he relieves my pain
Like blood flowing through my vein
Keeping me alive and feeding my brain
This feeling is so surreal
Feels like I'm drowning in the sea of love
But I don't care because he's . . .
                    My lover, my friend!

**Omolara Okunuga  (13)**
**Cliff Park High School, Gorleston**

# Since We Have Parted

Since we have parted, I don't feel the same.
There are times when I sit here,
And I can still hear you whispering my name.
Why did we separate when I really thought you cared?
I guess I misinterpreted what you said.
When I told you I'd always be there,
I really thought that you would care.
You didn't tell me what you'd done,
Until you had finished having fun.
You'd changed your mind, and that was it
You weren't ready for a relationship.
I thought we'd last longer, together at last,
But you would rather leave it in the past.
You like your nightclubs with different boys,
To try the different flavours for a worthy cause.
I was so close to giving you the most precious thing I have,
My love to you, but now I have it back.
I know I did not waste my time,
Because it was a worthwhile lesson,
I now know not to fall so easily.
Thank you for the feelings you had,
Just thank God, I'm not the father
Thank God, thank God!

**Jamie Lee Hollis  (15)**
**Cliff Park High School, Gorleston**

# Barney

Barney is my baby boy,
He gives me lots of love and joy,
He takes our dirty socks to Mum,
So she can put them in the washing drum,
Barney's a very clever lad,
But sometimes he can be very bad,
He sits beside our chairs at night,
Barks at nothing and gives us a fright,
When we got to bed at night,
He always comes in to say night-night,
In the morning, he's much more fun,
To wake us up he jumps on our tum,
It doesn't matter if he's good or bad,
He'll always be my beautiful, cheeky little lad.

**Nicola Stolworthy  (13)**
**Cliff Park High School, Gorleston**

# Life, So Bleak

Here comes Monday again,
Another school week,
How did I end up like this?
How'd my life become so bleak?

How does it feel
To be washed away?
To die piece by piece,
And day by day?

How'd this story,
Turn black and white?
It seems every friendship,
Becomes a fight.

I had a soul,
The other day,
I remember him screaming,
As he was dragged away.

How does it feel
To be the best
But never be noticed
And be below the rest?

Here comes Sunday again,
The end of another week,
Will I ever end like this?
Will I ever end so bleak?

**Kristofer Buchanan  (13)**
**Cliff Park High School, Gorleston**

# Silent Creature!

Heavy air, I can't breathe
This silent night won't let me free.
The quiet wind blows so long.
I try to be just as strong.
As a man that I once knew.
Non-greedy man, there are a few.
The skies say above my head,
I cannot rest, or go to bed.
No, I cannot turn my back.
For that is when it will attack.
Heavy air, hard to breathe.
This silent night won't let me see.

**Landan Beith (13)**
**Cliff Park High School, Gorleston**

# My Mates

My mates are friends,
We have great times,
We like to throw a party when our parents are not at home,
We loving getting drunk,
Hate the effect in the morning.

My mates are friends,
We all have sad times,
But we like to cheer each other up,
And we listen to what each other's got to say.

My mates are friends,
When we're out and about we like to have a bit of a run around
                                    and, of course, make trouble,
Just remember, think of the good times!

My mates become enemies,
We all fall out,
We fight and shout and get on everyone's wick,
But in the end, we're all good *mates!*

**Holly Chatten (14)**
**Cliff Park High School, Gorleston**

# Football

Football is a sport full of stars
Although some of them should be behind bars
Chelsea are rich
And deadly on the pitch.

A 'red card' and you're off!
The referee's a boff
The fans are chanting
And the goalposts are slanting.

The papers are full of player talk
But they'll soon shut up when they take 'the walk'.
Old managers are fired
And the new ones are hired.

You are three-nil down
Against Ipswich Town
The fans are booing your name in vain
As you're limping around in pain.

**Matt Kemp  (13)**
**Cliff Park High School, Gorleston**

# Test Torment

The boy spluttered as he woke up
knowing the day would be bad
as today he had a history test
with the horrible teacher, Miss Hagg.

The boy got to school very depressed
knowing he would fail Miss Hagg's test
by the time the lesson had come
from hand to foot he'd gone so numb.

The test started, he was so scared
all the others didn't care.
The test was finished, so much relief
now it was time to face the grief.

Miss Hagg called him in, he wondered if he had passed
unlike the rest of the class
100%, oh so great!
Miss Hagg said, 'Well done, mate!'

So he went home, no worries at all
congratulated by brother, Paul.
He was so happy, to bed he went
reflecting upon a day of greatness.

**Daniel Wright (14)**
**Cliff Park High School, Gorleston**

# Artists

An artist's thoughts ready to be spilled out on a canvas,
waiting to be made into a masterpiece.

His highly-skilled fingers itching to draw and,
finally, they're allowed to work their magic.

As the gentle bristles of the brush glide across the page,
like a knife cutting through butter,
a picture starts to emerge from the empty canvas
and the masterpiece starts to come along.

Finally, the masterpiece is finished
and it will now be shown in a gallery in all its glory
and the artist waits for more inspiration.

**Josh Leech  (13)**
**Cliff Park High School, Gorleston**

# The Mistake

'Is that a threat?'
I asked him
As the rain poured down
On my goosebumped skin.

He looked at me wide-eyed,
Through the thunder,
'You know, if you weren't a girl
You'd be six feet under.'

I stared back at him
In great disbelief
And slowly said through gritted teeth,
'I'm sorry.'

It rang through me
Like a bell in my head,
Repeating the words
That I had just said.

A smile on his face
He turned away.
Never again have I seen him
Since that day.

**Libby Cunningham  (13)**
**Cliff Park High School, Gorleston**

# Seasons

Spring is here
Soon it will be Easter
New life is born
And flowers grow.

Summer's here
Now we can party
Have late nights
And stay out late.

Now it is autumn
And the days are getting shorter
Nights are getting longer.

Winter is here
The snow is falling
Christmas is on the way
And a brand new year.

**Sarah Farrow  (13)**
**Cliff Park High School, Gorleston**

# Trapped

As I sit here all around me the shadows of my life,
Encircle and grip me by the throat,
Keep me down . . . broken . . . depressed,
I try to fight back,
To keep myself alive in the darkness,
I search for a lifeline but there is none,
I am alone with my deadly thoughts of the demons
Who plague my mind,
They bear down on me when I am alone,
It is the only time they are set free to wander,
But they do not go far - always returning to me when
I need them to be gone
One crushing blow after another they deliver to my insides,
Then the demoness herself rears her head and slams -
The final touch down onto what is left of my pitiful emotions,
There is nothing left for me now,
As the last of myself slips away into the black hole in my head,
I wonder if it will ever be released,
Then I see what is around me and realise there is no hope,
There is nothing but a void,
The place inside where I will forever be . . . trapped.

**James Goldsmith (16)**
**Cliff Park High School, Gorleston**

# Shoe Shoppin'!

I love shoe shoppin', it is so cool,
Round the shops I rule the school!
Green shoes,
Red shoes,
Black shoes,
Pink,
High shoes,
Flat shoes,
Any you can think!
Purple shoes,
Yellow shoes,
Orange shoes,
Blue.
Funky shoes,
Glitzy shoes,
And I need a drink!
I'm getting really tired now,
I think I'll head off home,
It's time for the curtain call, I'll take a bow.
All spent out, see you for now!

**Gemma Rimmer  (12)**
**Cliff Park High School, Gorleston**

# Going Home

Going home . . .
It's a wonderful sensation.
You pack your bags,
And walk out of class.

Going home . . .
It's a wonderful sensation.
You walk as fast as you can,
And get out of the school.

Going home . . .
It's a wonderful sensation.
You step on the bus
And think, *I'll be there in 20 minutes.*

Going home . . .
It's a wonderful sensation.
You friends are on the bus,
And you forget about school.

Going home . . .
It's a wonderful sensation.
You walk down the street,
And up the drive.

Going home . . .
It's a wonderful sensation.
Open the door, step inside,
And you feel perfect!

**Joseph O'Keefe (13)**
**Cliff Park High School, Gorleston**

# Professor Blinker

Professor Blinker
Worked so hard.
He built a bomb
In his backyard.

He lit the fuse,
Stood well back,
But not quite far enough,
Alack!

The bomb went off:
*Bang!*
Oh dear me
Professor Blinker
*RIP!*

**Kane Blyth (13)**
**Cliff Park High School, Gorleston**

# Ode To Nathan Sebastian

I look at you and my knees feel weak,
Everything about you makes my heart skip beats,
Your caramel eyes make me melt every time,
And I think I've got a crush on you,
Cos, damn, you're so fine,
I catch your eye and you smile at me,
But you turn away quick so your mates don't see,
You're older than me, three years, I think,
When I walk by you, my cheeks turn pink,
I missed you so much when you went away,
I missed you so much but you didn't stay,
You just left.

**Raffina Khalil  (13)**
**Cliff Park High School, Gorleston**

# Ribbons

Friends are always there for you,
In good times and in bad,
They laugh with you when you're happy,
And cry with you when you're sad,
True friends can get through anything,
Stand together in a storm,
And when they come out of it,
They will be stronger than ever before.

All friends are different,
And you like them all for different things,
A friend can support you,
And make you feel like you have wings,
When your friends are like your family,
You're there for each other no matter what,
You go out and have fun together,
And love them with all you've got.

Nothing can come between you,
And you work together as a team,
They'll support you if you fail,
And help you reach your dreams.

**Ishie Henderson  (13)**
**Cliff Park High School, Gorleston**

# Wedding Day

It was the perfect day for a wedding
The bride was dressed to kill
It happened, then she turned
And freaked for she saw her husband Bill
About to fall, she threw herself onto the window sill.

Someone was on a mission
On a mission to wreck her perfect day
She looked over and saw her husband
On the floor he lay
It was a scandal, what mindless person
Would do such a violent thing?
She cried and cried all the time, gazing at her wedding ring.

She found the enemy that brought death to her day
And murdered him
He prayed
The victim, Bill, tried to defend his wife
And ended up losing his own life!

**Jodie Smith (14)**
**Cliff Park High School, Gorleston**

# Till Death Do Us Part

The best words to say to a lady,
'Will you marry me?'
She then says, 'Yes,'
And imagines her dress,
And thinks, *what a perfect day this will be.*

He says to his bride,
'I will marry you with pride,
Just wait a little while,
Soon you'll walk down the aisle.

'Till death do us part,'
The vows read from the heart,
The guests they will cry,
From the happiness they feel inside.

'In the night at home,
You now won't spend alone,
I will keep you warm,
We will watch the sun rise at dawn.

Whenever you cry
I'll wipe the tears from your eyes,
For years and years,
I'll fight away all your fears,
I'll be there to hold your head up high,
To make any pain go by.'

**Kirsty Boult (13)**
**Cliff Park High School, Gorleston**

# Finding A Friend

The perfect wreck of a friendship,
I'm desperately seeking some trust,
Violent threats won't work anymore,
I'm already hurting too much.

People mindlessly laughing,
Talking and pointing at me,
My clothes and my hair are wrong,
Nobody cares for me.

I first saw her on Monday,
She came over and talked to me,
I've finally found a friend,
A girl who was lonely like me.

Now I have someone who likes me
To talk with and play with too.
She used to be scared like me,
Now she's just as happy too.

**Amy Steward  (13)**
**Cliff Park High School, Gorleston**

# Man On A Mission

A man on a mission,
Desperately seeking something he can never have,
The perfect scandal.

The victim,
The threat,
The sorrow.

Mindlessly wandering,
He sits,
In a reflection of his own regret.

A man on a mission,
Desperately seeking something he can never have,
The perfect scandal!

**Emma Campling  (13)**
**Cliff Park High School, Gorleston**

# Cheese!

Cheese is great,
Cheese is fun,
Cheese is the thing to fill your tum.

It can be big, it can be small,
It can be smelly,
But it could really hurt your belly.

Cheese is hard, cheese is soft,
Cheese is sometimes easily forgot.

It can be holey,
It can be off,
It can be on,
But try not to eat it when it looks really wrong.

So cheese is great,
Cheese is fun,
Cheese is the thing to fill your tum.

**Dale Nichols  (13)**
**Cliff Park High School, Gorleston**

# Her

I drown in a sea of want,
Of need.
Her presence could only save me.
My feelings are black text on a black page,
Illegible.
She is oblivious.
The truth struggles to escape,
The boundaries of the heart are strong.
If I could voice my desire,
If I could phrase my lust.
She is oblivious.

**Stuart Mileham  (13)**
**Cliff Park High School, Gorleston**

# Meant To Be

Down the winding path of love in life,
They'll always be together as man and wife,
It will not always be easy as they know,
But their love will always continue to grow.
A wish, a dream, that's now coming true,
There is always success in the things they do,
They've been through some hard times and fought them together,
This couple will last forever and ever.

**Tamsin Warnes (13)**
**Cliff Park High School, Gorleston**

# About A Girl

She wakes up in the morning,
Walking down the stairs she feels a dawning,
Plates smashing, glasses clanging,
All I hear is excess banging,
Is this compulsory, Lord?
She arrives,
Everything is silent except for the sighs,
She sits down and laughter starts,
Scattered around a broken heart.
Threatening sniggers run over her body,
Nasty scowls from everybody,
She's had enough.
She opens her bag,
No more people can call her a slag,
Sticks the needle in her arm,
Suddenly no one can do her any harm.
Five minutes later she's back again.
When will this stop? When?

**Michael Tooth  (13)**
**Cliff Park High School, Gorleston**

# Never Forgotten

Everything's so silent, every little thing reminds me of her.
She only went to the corner shop, it wasn't that far.
It was raining that day, I should never have let her go.
Was it my fault? I ask you. How was I to know?

I stand by the window waiting, waiting for her to come home.
Never leaving the house for anything, in case I miss the phone.
She'd never been late in from playing, never missed her tea.
I don't understand what happened, was it something to do with me?

I'd always let her go over the park and climb her favourite tree.
I've never believed in smothering her, everyone deserves to be free.
Although we had our ups and downs, everything always turned
out fine.
She'd always be my baby, my little girl, mine.

She doesn't hug me anymore or sit drawing in her room.
Where she walked there would be light, now she's gone,
there's only gloom.
I've left her things just how they were, including her bedroom.
You never know, although it's been two months, I know she'll
come home soon!

**Emma Farrow  (14)**
**Cliff Park High School, Gorleston**

# The Wedding

The wedding was ruined,
Glancing at her violet reflection,
She stared at the grotesque vision,
The party no longer the mission.

The sensational bride became a threat,
Dressed as the victim,
Mindlessly worrying,
Watching society fall

The day was more than perfect
The food was scrumptious,
The distant relatives rumoured? A scandal
Small boys pouting as if it was an ordeal

The groom was a wreck
His friends hearing his sorrows
Scarred for life by women,
The wedding was ruined.

**Christopher Davis (14)**
**Cliff Park High School, Gorleston**

# Moving House

I feel so alone,
And I wanna go home,
I miss it so much,
I never wanted to go,
I sit upstairs cryin',
Cos my memories are dyin',
I feel so alone,
And I wanna go home.

I didn't wanna go,
They made me leave,
I feel so low,
I wipe my eyes on my sleeve,
No one understands me,
As I start to cry,
I never really said goodbye,
To my life.

Some people may laugh,
And think that I am daft,
I've gotta move on,
Cos everyone's gone,
It's so empty now,
I'm still wondering how,
It happened so quick,
And it makes me feel sick.

I hate my new house,
It's not my home,
I'm going away,
I can't stay,
I hate my life now,
I don't like it one bit,
I sit up all night,
Waitin' for the light.

**Melanie-Jo Pearson (14)**
**Cliff Park High School, Gorleston**

# Misinterpreted

We all thought you were happy,
But we soon found out the truth,
Your eyes reflected a secret,
That we didn't want to hear.

Your sorrow hidden by a smile,
Your pain hidden by your laughter,
We accepted you, you accepted us,
We had the perfect trust.

Then you met another friend,
As sharp as life could be,
You wore your scars with pride,
Until one day you'd gone,
Death had crept upon you!

**Karina Savill  (14)**
**Cliff Park High School, Gorleston**

# Drugged

Cold, still
Totally ruined
Lying dead
Like a ruined wreck.
Falling mindlessly
Through desperate sorrow.
A reflective vision
Like a perfect mission
Grotesque
Silent
Worried.

Children crying
People dying
Blood running silently
Down a brick wall
Still, cold.

**Rosemarie Young  (14)**
**Cliff Park High School, Gorleston**

# Christmas That Year

Desperately seeking an answer for why?
Why he didn't love me anymore?
Why did I fall from daughter to scum?
Christmas that year was perfect sorrow
What have I done?
I've ruined our love
And at this time of year, families and joy indeed,
He hates me now,
The last three years in mental violence and thoughts
What have I done?
Dad, I'm sorry.

**Gemma Groom (14)**
**Cliff Park High School, Gorleston**

# Deadly

Deadly like a dark scorpion,
From its sharp sting.

Deadly like a gripping bite,
From a venomous snake.

Deadly as a light touch,
From a small black widow.

Deadly as an evil eye,
From a creepy old man.

Deadly as the scorching sun,
If it were to hit the skin of a vampire.

Deadly as a dark dream,
Haunting you from life to death.

**Ben Andrews  (13)**
**Cliff Park High School, Gorleston**

# Love And Weddings

Love is all around us everywhere you look.
Many people like it but I think it's yuck.
All the kissing, getting married and things,
spending loads of money on little engagement rings.
When the wedding is finally over
there are cheers and speeches and people doing silly things.
The only bit I like about weddings is the cake and the beer,
getting on the dance floor and doing my own thing.
When you get home from the wedding everybody is tired,
you strip naked and jump into bed.
You turn out the light.
Rest your head.
Close your eyes and tomorrow will be a surprise.
40 years later if you're still alive, you celebrate by having a
big party for your time.

**Adam Newman (14)**
**Cliff Park High School, Gorleston**

# Suffering

I'm deeply suffering
The pain, he left me
Some anger growing in my mind
My feelings
*Hate*
*Love*
    And *pain.*

He's deeply suffering
He suffers because I suffer
Memories of good times *haunting* him
He wishes he hadn't done it.

We're in a bad situation
Wanting to get back together
It's driving us insane.

**Ben Dorrin  (13)**
**Cliff Park High School, Gorleston**

# Suffering

She had suffered the same fate I had,
Soon it will be my turn,
After she died I felt like I had no one,
I was in a world of my own.

She wouldn't have died if I were there,
My life is now turning the corner,
She would have lived like me,
She died without compassion.

She had to leave me,
If she had to leave me, not like that,
I feel like I can't go on like this,
I need her with me.

She couldn't stand me any longer,
That is why she died,
I know I have to get over her death,
I am suffering without her.

**Jak Lewis Sargeant (14)**
**Cliff Park High School, Gorleston**

# Suffering

Suffering is pain
Suffering is war
Suffering is insecure
Suffering . . .
Suffering is poor
Suffering is closing the door
Suffering . . .

**Leon Riches (13)**
**Cliff Park High School, Gorleston**

# Beautiful

Beautiful
Can describe anyone.
It can't describe me.
I'm different in every single way.
Like celebrities,
They worry about how they look.
Not everyone has to look great or beautiful.
Just be
          Normal . . . be . . .
Yourself,
Don't think you're ugly,
Everyone is beautiful . . .
In different ways!

**Harriet Wheeler  (13)**
**Cliff Park High School, Gorleston**

# Autumn

When autumn breeze comes calling,
Autumn leaves start falling,
Up in the trees,
Then on the ground
Leaves spinning all around,
Blossom starts to bloom
Here comes their awful doom
Swishing and swaying from side to side
Just like the sea's dreadful tide.

**Emma Miller  (12)**
**Cliff Park High School, Gorleston**

# Love

Love isn't a word,
It's a meaning.
Love is what you feel,
It's a warm feeling.
You get it when you see someone,
Someone close to the heart,
Someone that you wish no harm to,
Only the people that hurt them.
Love is a person,
Gentle, soft, harmless,
She has a soft, sweet voice
And makes you tingle when she speaks.
Love isn't a word,
It's a meaning.

**Cameron Chalk  (12)**
**Cliff Park High School, Gorleston**

# Dark

Dark is a ghost
Which can only be seen at nine o'clock.
Dark is a killer that can't be arrested.
The dark takes over your soul
Covering your body like a piece of coal.
Dark can take your life in a second.
That's all it takes . . .

**Mitchell Park  (13)**
**Cliff Park High School, Gorleston**

# Suffering

A cruel suffering world,
People hurt,
People suffering,
They need help,
But there is no one to help them in this suffering world.

People made to suffer by the world,
People making people suffer,
People have suffered and are still suffering,
The world is suffering.

**Sam Davy (12)**
**Cliff Park High School, Gorleston**

# Painful

Painful,
When I fall and graze my knee,
When I get stung by a bee.

Painful,
When I lose at my favourite games,
When someone laughs and calls me names.

Painful,
When I hear someone cry,
When someone that I knows, dies.

Painful,
When I hear a bone crack,
When I hear what's going on in Iraq.

It's painful.

**Samantha Joseph  (12)**
**Cliff Park High School, Gorleston**

# This World

People suffering in this world,
Children starving in this world,
Governments laughing in this world,
Little bothers us in this world,
Pollution, a problem in this world,
Evil lurks in this world,
War is life in this world,
Nothing's perfect in this world.

**Joe Gunton-Jones (12)**
**Cliff Park High School, Gorleston**

# Death

Death will come to everyone,
There isn't a single being that it won't.
Be it illness, age or the worst of all, murder,
And who are we to resist?

The day will come when you stand,
Knocking on the Grim Reaper's door,
And he will then engulf you,
In the everlasting blackness alone for evermore.

That's the moment you regret,
Your wrong-doings when alive,
Your evilness, your hatred,
Add up and bring you down.

Down with a crash and thump!
Alone with only black for company.
Flames licking at your ears,
And your punishment now complete.

But despite your wrongs and hatred,
You'll be missed all the same,
But there's no going back now,
The grief, they seek revenge.

**Guy Dent  (12)**
**Cliff Park High School, Gorleston**

# Troubled Waters

Troubled waters,
The deep shimmering sea,
Filled with pollution,
The sea drowning in chemicals,
Slowly dying,
The troubled waters,
Not to be a part of the future,
To be replaced
With an unclean puddle,
No fish left,
We'll be living off GM crops,
And animals who have spent their short lives in cages,
They leave it for the generations of the future to deal with,
Let their sons and daughters deal with it,
Let them never know nature,
Children die from drinking polluted water,
Not polluted by them, by westerners,
Troubled waters.

**Joe Blance  (13)**
**Cliff Park High School, Gorleston**

# Dark

In the dark I sit alone
Am I invisible or something?
Can no one see me?
It's getting late now.
No one's looking for me.
No one cares!
I hate being alone.
It's so depressing.
Do you think they've forgotten me?
Did they leave me here on purpose?
Listen, someone's coming!
No, it's not my mum.
I really loved her.
I guess she didn't love me.
Should I cry
Or is there no point?
I'm not very old you know.
I won't survive long.
I'm small as well.
I can't get my own food.
I'm not sure how.
Will they ever come and get me?
I'll die without them.
I need to hold them.
I need to feel their hearts beat.
I need their arms around me.
Someone help, I can't survive alone.
Do people hate me that much?
What do people have against puppies?

**Elise Farrow  (12)**
**Cliff Park High School, Gorleston**

# Ugly Truth

No one wants to hear it,
No one wants to believe it,
No one teaches it,
But everyone learns it.

The ugly truth is everywhere,
It's on TV, the radio,
And everywhere you look.

The ugly truth is people hate each other,
Sometimes I've had enough,
I hate the way the world is,
I want to get rid of the ugly truth.

**Michaela Guthrie  (12)**
**Cliff Park High School, Gorleston**

# Dark

*Shock!* It hits you and it's cold,
*Bang!* It hits you and it's old.
*Slam!* It hits you and it's strange,
*Whack!* It hits you and it's the range.
*Wham!* It hits you and it's a pain,
*Smash!* It hits you and it's the cane.
*Bash!* It hits you and it's *dark!*

**Sinéad Munden (13)**
**Cliff Park High School, Gorleston**

# Money

Hatred pours from a single pound
Greed is the cause of this coin or note
Where is the serenity in this obsession?
If you have it, you can use it to gloat
When it's gone your world drifts away
It's money that leads your world astray.

**Amy Nicholson  (13)**
**Cliff Park High School, Gorleston**

# Free

Am I free . . . ?
Free to be me?
Free to love, free to hate?
*No.*
I'm trapped
In a never-ending nightmare,
On and on.
*No,*
I'm not free,
Not free to be me.
I've never been free.

**Annie Hunt  (13)**
**Cliff Park High School, Gorleston**

# Depressed

I hate the world,
Everyone is so damn depressed,
I hate the world,
Why can't they have fun?
I hate the world . . .

I hate my life,
I'm all alone,
I hate my life,
They're all so dull,
I hate my life . . .

I hate them all,
Why can't we laugh?
I hate them all,
Laughing's in the past,
I hate them all . . .

I'm not depressed,
Just misunderstood . . .
I'm not depressed,
It's all of you,
Just leave me alone . . .

**Andrew Stamp (12)**
**Cliff Park High School, Gorleston**

# Friendship

Our friendship is so fine
Our friendship will never end
Never in our time
Because you are my friend
I remember so well
As we walked down the road
The secrets we told each other
Our friendship will never end
I remember times we spent
Feeding horses, Reggie and Ben
We'd sit on the hay
The same day each year
And declare our friendship won't end
As we laughed
We talked about
How we would always be friends forever
I've known you so long now
I know our friendship won't end.

**Verity Howard  (12)**
**Cliff Park High School, Gorleston**

# TV

'Mind-boggling, brain-rotting rubbish.'
That's what my mum says to me about TV.

'Super sport, fantastic films, excellent entertainment.'
That's what my dad says to me about TV.

'The Simpsons, Malcolm In The Middle and Robot Wars.'
That's what my brother says to me about TV.

Me! I don't understand TV.
After all I'm only three!

**Thomas Jermy (12)**
**Cliff Park High School, Gorleston**

# Red

Red is anger
Red is rage
Which people feel
At every age.

Red is blood
Red is hate
Maybe over
Something we ate

Red is fire
Red is flame
Red is warmth
Which I want to gain.

**Jennifer Coles  (12)**
**Cliff Park High School, Gorleston**

# Hair

Brown, blonde, ginger, black, grey, white.
What's your hair like?
Blonde highlights, brown highlights, blue highlights,
pink highlights, green highlights.
What's your hair like?
Dyed purple, red, orange, yellow, green, blue
magenta, black, pink and white.
What's your hair like?
Straight, curly, crimped, frizzy, spiky,
messy, long or short.
What's your hair like?

**Sarah Griffin  (12)**
**Cliff Park High School, Gorleston**

# Dark

Huddled all alone in the dark
Sitting there all lonely in the dark
Kept in a corner in the dark
On the stone-cold floor in the dark
Listening to the silence in the dark
Closing my eyes in the dark.

I called her name. No answer.
I ran for miles ahead.
I ran into a flash of lightning
Nothing to be said.
There was a sign, a symbol, a mark
All this while kept in the dark!

**Amelia Elizabeth Brooke Lennon**
**Cliff Park High School, Gorleston**

# Tragedy

What is a tragedy?
Is it good? Is it bad?
What are the effects of a tragedy?
Are they good? Are they bad?
When will the tragedy end?
When will the tragedy happen?
Has it happened?
What will happen to me if there is a tragedy?
I wouldn't know. I was killed. Was that in a tragedy?

**Nick Mobbs  (12)**
**Cliff Park High School, Gorleston**

# Accident

What a terrible accident,
He tried to get out but he couldn't,
As it came off the tracks,
The alarm sounded loud,
There was an almighty crash,
And a sudden crack and bash.

The police siren was moaning,
And all the injured were groaning,
The tracks had all buckled,
And things were going crazy,
The spectators were gathering,
And nothing . . . was travelling!

**Toby Harrison  (12)**
**Cliff Park High School, Gorleston**

# The Star Bride's Wedding

The star bride worries for a ruined wedding
Because a violent society falls
In trembling sorrow
For her wedding, she is dressed for the occasion
But her mind is wrecked
The threat upon her wedding is great
Death is in the woman's mind
But it's just another delicious classic star bride wedding.

**Aaron Shuckford (13)**
**Cliff Park High School, Gorleston**

# Feelings

As I look mindlessly
Staring at the woman
The centre of my life
My future bride
Waiting to be snatched.

Love is like stars
That twinkle violently
In each other's hearts
Just waiting to feel that sorrow
In the ruined souls of everyone.

When that wound has healed
It's like a vision
A reflection
Of a threat forced upon you.

**Benjamin Harrison  (13)**
**Cliff Park High School, Gorleston**

# Who Was She?

As I stood there
Locked in some kind of sensation
I wondered who she was
That reflection of beauty
She was perfect
Just scrumptious
Then I saw him
I was ruined.

**Danny James  (13)**
**Cliff Park High School, Gorleston**

# The Rap

Perfect sorrow
Ruined wedding
Simply scrumptious
Violent death
Desperately seeking
Animal sensation
Defended victim
Classic mission.

**Billy Smith  (13)**
**Cliff Park High School, Gorleston**

# An Unhappy Wedding

A perfect wedding and a ruined party.
A victim for the death, and a worry for the funeral.
A sensational vision of the classic party.
The sorrow, the worry for the poor animals.
The man was ruined, wrecked and really worried.

**Laura Docwra  (13)**
**Cliff Park High School, Gorleston**

# Poetry

I am a star
I've been a bride
I've been partying
I've been cheeky
I'm not that perfect.

I've fallen over
I love animals
I've dressed up
I do trust you
You're simply the best

There is a wreck
I'll always defend my friends
I love weddings
I've been a bride all my life.

**Becky Louise Lumb (13)**
**Cliff Park High School, Gorleston**

# A Mystery Bride

A perfect bride, with a scrumptious scandal
Desperately seeking a violent death.
The big day here for her sensational wedding
But also for a delicious death.

**Kallie Rollinson  (13)**
**Cliff Park High School, Gorleston**

# The Scam

The scam was so perfect,
The scam was so simple,
The scam was so scrumptious, how could it fail?
The victim never guessed death was so close,
If only that wretched woman hadn't got so close,
I would have succeeded if it hadn't been for that ghost.

**Joshua Beckett  (14)**
**Cliff Park High School, Gorleston**

# Why Should I Care?

I just cannot be bothered anymore
Why should I care?
This doesn't make sense
Why should I care?
I can't write poetry,
Why should I care?
You don't have to read this so
Why should I care?

**Ben Cook (15)**
**Cliff Park High School, Gorleston**

# Nightmare

I run, I stop
I turn, I look
I rest, I look
I sweat, I pant
This place is unsafe
It's loose, it's free
It's hungry and real
It's never been real
Before it was just a dream.
I remember a night
Of horror and shock
I remember a dream
Of a monster and me
The monster hates me
And now it's after me
A childhood dream
          released.

**Craig Mallindine  (15)**
**Cliff Park High School, Gorleston**

# My World?

There is a blue elephant juggling planets
On one, the mountains are as purple as the sunset
The trees are pink
The world is so happy
And there is a constant rainbow.
On another it is all black.
Black like night.
Black like death.
Black as evil.
It is full of red fire.
Everyone is in pain.
Then there is my world - Earth.
We are not perfect
But we are not evil.
We are not fully happy
But we are not totally sad.
We are no angels
But there is no demon here.
But what if these worlds were to vanish?
Where would all the people go?
Where would all the animals be?
What about me?
There would be a hole in my heart
As big as the hole in the galaxy.
Would the elephant abandon us?
Why shouldn't he?
We would abandon him.
My world.
Don't abandon peace for hatred.
Don't abandon love for hate.
It's not my world - it's ours.
Don't destroy Earth.

**Catherine Butler (15)**
**Cliff Park High School, Gorleston**

# Blue Elephant

A blue elephant was raiding the pantry,
But all he could find was some tantree.
So he cooked it and cooked it until it went black,
Though he wanted a meal not a petty snack.
He decided to go shopping for some tasty food,
But he didn't realise he'd gone out in the nude.

**Chris Morris (15)**
**Cliff Park High School, Gorleston**

# The Child That Would Have Been

Outside, the birds and other animals were going berserk.
They say they can sense disaster looming,
Like before earthquakes and the sort.
Inside the farmer and his wife are together,
Like one body,
One form,
Crying for their lives that they are about to lose.
Confessions.
They tell each other their secrets.
And for a minute they wonder what this child would have been like.
They hear the rumbling as the world around them begins to collapse.
They cry again,
This time, not for their own lives, but each other's and the child
that would have been.

**Rory McDaid (15)**
**Cliff Park High School, Gorleston**

# My Life

Suddenly, all of a sudden,
Instead, before my eyes,
My life, my past, present and future,
My twisted words sounding unfamiliar with myself.

Instead, words upon twisted words,
An angel, a hypocrite, a devil,
Determination to make sense,
My life before my eyes.

'My life' printed in big haunting letters,
I dare to look,
'Strictly Confidential' in small hypertext, peripherals and binaries,
My confidential information exposed . . .

Permission granted,
My past, without a care in the world,
My present, making no sense at all,
My future, saving the world before the galaxy collapses.

Questioning the future.

**Trystan Potter  (15)**
**Cliff Park High School, Gorleston**

# Subject

In English we had to write a poem
For this competition called 'Poetry In Motion'.
I was thinking about Michael Owen
Or witches and their potions.

So I came up with an idea
Of a poem in fear
All different things to write about.
So many choices so which one to pick?

I pick you, the one I'm writing
It's about you and the fun things you do.
You do things, saying words,
Expressing yourself.

*Poetry in motion!*

**Jessica Falco (13)**
**Cliff Park High School, Gorleston**

# My Grandad

His home was warm,
he was kind,
he was not hard to find.

He'd be up a ladder
up a tree
making a den just for me.

He'd share his sweets
give us kisses
help us first and then himself.

His life ended suddenly
which was really upsetting
but at least I know everyone
has at least one cherished memory!

**Aimee Grand (13)**
**Cliff Park High School, Gorleston**

# Peace

Yippee! Hooray!
The war is over
Everybody's looking
For their four-leafed clover.
Houses are trashed
People are killed
Not like normal
When people are chilled.
You look around
At the ground
Scared and alone
*Not* safe and sound.

**Amanda Barker  (13)**
**Cliff Park High School, Gorleston**

# Rugby Union

R ough, fast and skilful.
U nion is much better than league.
G oals and touch downs get you points.
B odies get battered and bruised.
Y oung people always keen.

U pset if you lose, but you can improve.
N ever give up, keep trying your best.
I n games, you have to be on your toes.
O ver the post, that's what the conversions are.
N ever trying to let them win.

**Callum Ruane  (13)**
**Cliff Park High School, Gorleston**

# I Sit Here And Cry

Nobody knows just how I feel.
I sit here and cry,
I want some friends but nobody wants me,
So I sit here and cry.

I get bullied at school,
I sit here and cry,
But nobody listens,
So I sit here and cry.

But now I've died,
I don't cry, I don't cry,
But I hear laughs around me,
I still sit here and cry.

**Jade Barber  (13)**
**Cliff Park High School, Gorleston**

# Night

The darkness is coming.
Slowly creeping.
The sun is dying.
People weeping.
The shadows grow longer.
The night gets deeper.
Return from slumber
*To haunt the newcomer!*

**Kevin Blossfeldt  (13)**
**Cliff Park High School, Gorleston**

# The Perfect Bride

The perfect bride, at her perfect wedding,
The white, the cake, the church,
The groom.

The perfect wedding started so well,
Classic, just as she'd dreamed,
Just as she'd hoped.

As she floated down the aisle it all went wrong,
As a violent storm struck,
The lights went out.

The church was destroyed
And the wedding ruined.
The wind blew her hair,
And the veil left for the sky, left for the moon.

She was desperately seeking her star of a groom,
And she mindlessly ran to their home,
Her home.

The vision of death hung over her head,
Her party ruined, her groom lost.

She fell to her knees and cried until her reflection
Showed in a puddle on the floor.

She believed she could not go on,
Her groom lost,
The perfect bride!

**Liam Nudd (14)**
**Cliff Park High School, Gorleston**

# A Dog Is For Life

We've been locked up in this shed now
Since we were eight months old
We've been moved around a lot in cardboard boxes
In and out of houses
But we finally got placed in this terrible place
Never get fed
Never get walked
We live here all eight of us
Dad's dead, Mum's nearly gone
Nobody can hear us crying
We finally see some light
But it's when we've gone up to Heaven.

**Megan Crane  (13)**
**Cliff Park High School, Gorleston**

# Tobias

My dog's called Tobias,
Tobias is his name,
He barks all day and sleeps all night,
And he's always a pain!
He barks at the cat next door,
And he'll bark for evermore,
He's small and clean,
He's a barking machine,
And he'll make your ears sore!

**Phil Cox  (13)**
**Cliff Park High School, Gorleston**

# Aliens

Aliens have landed
Landed on Earth
They are green
Green all over
They are after
After all of us
They have got some
Some of us
They have captured
Captured us
We are prisoners
Prisoners to them
We have one night
One night to live
We hear them
Them speaking
They want us dead
Dead to the bone
Aliens have landed
Landed on Earth.

**Oliver Gatley (13)**
**Cliff Park High School, Gorleston**

# Him

When I woke, he was gone.
Disappeared.
Disappeared out of my life.
Out of my life forever.
I wish.
Oh I wish I could spend my life with him.
He would not believe me.
Believe I didn't do it.
He would not trust me.
Trust me for something I didn't do.
How?
How can I get him to believe me?
'I can never trust you,' he said, it rings,
Rings in my head, over and over.
I will spend my nights alone.
Alone with no one to hold.
Hold in my arms when I'm cold or feeling really sad.
I wish.
Oh I wish he would come back!

**Siobhan Mitchell  (14)**
**Cliff Park High School, Gorleston**

# Star, My Dog

My dog is named Star,
He is the best.
His favourite thing is the car,
He hates to have a rest.

My dog eats a lot,
Munching at his food.
Scoffing it down, like that's all he's got.
He can be so rude.

Star loves his walks
And never wants to come back.
He'll bark and talk,
Some day he'll get the knack.

He loves to play
With all his toys,
Out in the garden on a sunny day
And to bark at all the boys.

That is my dog,
Star
For
You!

**Kimberley Anderson  (13)**
**Cliff Park High School, Gorleston**

# France

F riendly neighbours,
R unning around to make you feel at home.
A nyone's welcome.
N ever want to leave.
C ome to France,
E veryone has a good time!

**Leah Saunders  (13)**
**Cliff Park High School, Gorleston**

# Gran Canaria

G reat place for holidays,
R ain never comes so it's,
A lways sunny and hot,
N othing to worry about,

C an sunbathe all day,
A qua parks a great day out,
N obody can complain,
A dorable beaches,
R avishing seas,
I t's just,
A totally great place.

**Lacie Pammen (13)**
**Cliff Park High School, Gorleston**

# Why?

She seemed so troubled,
She seemed so wise,
She seemed troubled,
Wondering why?

She walked along,
She walked so wide,
She walked along,
Wondering why?

She has no future,
She has no life,
She has no message,
Wondering why?

She is so lonely,
She is so sad,
She is so angry
Wondering why?
Why?

**Sharmain Webb  (13)**
**Cliff Park High School, Gorleston**

# Going Out!

I'm going out for the night on the town,
My friend said I look like a clown.

Putting all my make-up on,
And curling my hair with my tongs.

Just got time to fix my hair,
Before I run and hit the air.

I look in the mirror and think
*God, I look young,*
But after all,
      Girls just wanna have fun!

**Zoey Beddow (14)**
**Cliff Park High School, Gorleston**

# Mysterious

M ysterious places
Y es they are real
S pooky settings
T he zombies attacking you
E erie castles
R eal monsters
I nvisible ghosts
O vergrown witches putting you under a spell
U nnatural beings
S piders.

**Lydia Collins (13)**
**Cliff Park High School, Gorleston**

# Melanie

M ental sometimes
E nergetic
L ovely always
A ngry, never
N ormal, I wish
I am me and no one else
E verlasting friend.

**Melanie Debbage  (13)**
**Cliff Park High School, Gorleston**

# America

A nnoying voices
M aniac driving
E verything so big
R acing cops
I n the city.
C haos everywhere
A nd all around.

**Alex Harvey (13)**
**Cliff Park High School, Gorleston**

# Skeletons!

S limy skin
K nocking on the door
E erie happenings
L egless ghosts
E verything scary
T he living dead
O pen the closet
N othing appears
S creaming so bad.

**Nicola Gray (13)**
**Cliff Park High School, Gorleston**

# The Mess

Sorry, fresh, real
spontaneous, sad, death
life, fun, do
don't, live, lame
lass, lad, lamp
surreal, anti-disestablishmentarianism
scrumptious, tasty, yummy,
Mummy, Daddy, extraordinary,
out of the ordinary, desperate, separate
tractor, fish.
Fish?
Tree, stuck, sane,
insane, strange, hallucinogenic
obscene, coliseum, gladius
gladiator, gradient, grim
dark, swotty, supreme
holy, angry, strong
weak, kind, realism
degenerate, sadistic, ballistic
grand, big, ginormous
gigantic xylophone
xylophone?
Lead, fed, red
bed, said, dead

ominously

extreme!

**Adam Khan (14)**
**Cliff Park High School, Gorleston**

# The Animal

I lie here in a steely cage,
Under the moonlit sky.
A victim from the velvet cover,
That holds right over me.
I lie here simply waiting.
Can someone set me free?

I lie here as a tortured animal,
Falling through the darkness.
I lie here under the black dressed sky,
As a wreck and failing ruin.
I'm turning to insanity,
So please just set me free!

A reflection of my former self,
Waiting for the dawn.
A hunting, lurching predator,
Waiting for the time.
I see the way that I must go,
Now I become free.

**Helen Richardson  (13)**
**Cliff Park High School, Gorleston**

# A Friend In Need

A friend in need,
A friend indeed,
A friend upset,
A friend perplexed.
A friend with a secret,
A friend that's a keeper,
A friend that hurts,
A friend that learns.
A friend that's stupid,
A friend acting Cupid.
A friend that shocks,
A friend that mocks,
A friend that worries,
A friend that hurries.

A friend that's black,
A friend that's white,
A friend that cries every night.

A friend in need,
A friend indeed!

**Michelle Reeve (13)**
**Cliff Park High School, Gorleston**

# My Wedding Day Not! Ha Ha!

The perfect wedding, the perfect day
Angelic and peaceful

Dressed to impress
She looked like an angel

She looked in the mirror
What did she see . . . ?

She saw an angel
She blew us all away

It started to rain
She said to herself,
'I won't let the rain ruin my big day'

She received a letter saying
'You better watch yourself'

She had been thinking about the threat she got
*How dare they try to wreck my wedding day?*

She said to herself
'I'm at death's door.'

**Lucy Haylock  (13)**
**Cliff Park High School, Gorleston**

# Woman On A Mindless Mission

Violent bride desperately seeking grotesque victim,
For perfect marriage,
Must reflect grandfather,
And have a simply scrumptious death,
For simple sensations,
Death must be dressed for politeness,
Confusing? Yes,
Make sense? No,
Puzzling world isn't it?

**James Clifford  (15)**
**Cliff Park High School, Gorleston**

# Everything

Every mission holds a threat
Every threat has a victim
Every victim has an enemy
Every enemy has a plot
Every plot includes a death
Every death takes a life
Everything has an end.

**Laura Rumsby  (14)**
**Cliff Park High School, Gorleston**

# The Party

She came up the path,
Like a shining star, dressed.
She looked like a beautiful bride,
Waiting for the party to begin, she sat,
And noticed the table perfectly laid,
With the delicious food, staring into her face,
It felt like a sensation that would never end.

**Sarah Davey  (12)**
**Cliff Park High School, Gorleston**

# Love

Oh how I love, *love,*
It's like a white dove,
As it goes through the trees,
Oh how I love, *love,*
Like a dolphin going through the waves
Love is like a roller coaster,
Up, down, side to side, all around,
Oh, how I love, *love,*
It's like the sky,
Blue, black,
Good times, bad times.
Oh how I love, *love,*
It's like a cloud,
Here, there, everywhere,
Oh how I love, *love,*
Love can be everlasting,
Oh how I love, *love!*

**Sophie Hazelden (12)**
**Cliff Park High School, Gorleston**

# Innocence

I don't believe in innocence anymore
It's ruined.
What kind of animal?
My vision of trust and forgiving,
It's ruined.

**Grace Porter (8)**
**Cliff Park High School, Gorleston**

# At The Park

The boy went in the park
Went on the already-swinging swing.
Jumped on a jumbo jet.
Called his mum,
Hands were numb.
It was cold,
Cold as snow
Saw a dog
Thought it was a hog.
Mum ran over - just got back from Dover
Ended up brown
She'd seen the whole town.

**Luke Wassell  (12)**
**Cliff Park High School, Gorleston**

# Our Victory

13th April 1966, a mission was to be completed,
The stars above would be pleased
For the Earth also, would be pleased.
We went up, up and up,
Into the sky, then into space.
It was a one-off chance to complete
The mission, for us, for the stars.
We were in space now,
We had relaxed, soon the big throttle pushed us into space.
We were *free!* We were off on a journey
To the stars, to the moon. For our people
It came to the day when all hope was dwindling for us.
Down, down we went to the surface of the star.
A twirling star we were on. A twinkle of light!
It was time for men to make it a big day.
'One small step for man, one big leap for mankind!'
Before we knew it, we were back -
Back home with our families.

**Joshua Coles (12)**
**Cliff Park High School, Gorleston**

# A Suicide Imitation

My bare hands clutch at the knife
That holds her fate.
The mirror image stands still.
It's not me though, but her
Is that what you see in me?

Stepping into the darkness, into black
My mind - insane with revenge
My eyes only seeing crimson colours
This moment will last forever

She stands there, waiting for you
The wind blowing on the snowy clifftop
She hears Death whisper in her ear
To her I am Death. I am the end.

Step forward. She slips and you call
Again, you want to protect her. Not me!
Anger! Fear! Then she falls into
The heart of Hell. My heart.

**Kelly-Marie Tuck  (15)**
**Cliff Park High School, Gorleston**

# Cats

Cats hid and made mighty spells
While their dishes fell, like ringing bells
In places deep, where dark things sleep
In hollow baskets beneath the smells.

On human laps they are strung
The fluffy balls  on string, they hung
The roaring fire looked like twisted wire
They nap through the light of the moon and sun.

For over the misty villages cold
To houses deep and cottages old
We must await the rise of day
They seek their food like it's enchanted gold.

They have been here since the ancient lord
Many came in a furry hoard
Strong and tough, mice they caught
To hide in a stomach like a sword.

**Catherine Barlett  (12)**
**Cliff Park High School, Gorleston**

# War Hammer

W ar was inevitable
A nd destiny
R oyal lords commanding troops

H ails of fire overhead
A rrows from bowmen
M illions of troops
M arch over the battlefield
E very weapon firing
R eal war is *here!*

**Justin Klausner (13)**
**Cliff Park High School, Gorleston**

# Seasons

When spring is here
the animals start to appear
and everything is calm and quiet.

When summer is coming
we all start running
along the sandy shore.

When autumn's here
I start to shed a tear
at the cooling wind and rain.

When winter's coming
we all start humming
the Christmas tunes and songs.

**Laura Black (12)**
**Cliff Park High School, Gorleston**

# Death Of A First Love

I threw myself upon my bed
And cried and cried and cried
And crying thus, my heart has said
It were better had I died.

True love is all at once, too hard
Too different to behold
It kills your dreams, it splits your heart
And tramples on your soul.

But senses speak and life proceeds
To everyone and each
The cry goes up and all repeat
'There are more pebbles on the beach!'

**Victoria Leggett  (15)**
**Cliff Park High School, Gorleston**

# Best Friends

Best friends are there to laugh and cry,
Best friends are there to be by your side.
Best friends to me are meant to be
They talk to you and set you free.

Our friendship here is so deep,
If you left me I'd sit and weep.
If you have any problems, then just say,
'I'll be right here, all the way.'

I don't know what I'd do without
My life would be just one big doubt.

Best friends hooray!

**Kayleigh Jane Bartram (15)**
**Cliff Park High School, Gorleston**

# War

Lives are lost
Hopes have vanished,
Hearts are broken
Fear is surrounding us
Just for pride.

Countries collapsing,
Buildings falling down.
Everyone's crying,
Taking their last breath
Just for land.

They fire rockets
Aiming to end lives of the innocent.
Just for . . .

**Abdul Hamza-Aly  (13)**
**Cliff Park High School, Gorleston**

# The Skier

As the skier rides down the snow
White powder spraying everywhere,
Everyone likes to have a go
But it's like a really, big dare.

As the skier does a 360 jump,
He is gliding through the air.
The skier ends up in a large slump,
The crowd are watching in despair.

The skier swoops down, left to right,
Taking over the snowploughs,
The skier skis with almighty might,
Then he ends up in a bed of flowers.

People complain how fast he's going,
'It's not my fault, I'm just too fast!'
The people are staring; anger is flowing,
Two weeks later, he's in an arm-cast!

**Callum Connell  (12)**
**Cliff Park High School, Gorleston**

# Nature

Nature, nature,
The gruesome yet beautiful nature.
The birds in the sky
The horse in the field,
A little bear cub looks friendly and cute -
But as for their parents, they're real brutes.

Nature, nature,
The gruesome yet beautiful nature.
The woodpecker's tap
And the lion's roar.

Nature, nature,
The gruesome yet beautiful nature.
How long will we have it for?
The trees are being cut down,
Because companies claim they need the land.
The animals' habitat is being wrecked.
Is this what you call beautiful nature?
So the lions are predators,
They kill other animals -
But so do we!

Nature, nature,
The gruesome yet beautiful nature.
If we don't do more to preserve it -
We won't have it anymore.
Is that what we want?

**Andrew Allcock  (13)**
**Cliff Park High School, Gorleston**

# Blue

Blue is icy cold,
On as crisp, winter day.
Where snow flutters onto the ground
For children who like to play.

Blue is depression,
Like tears running down from your eyes.
You feel lonely and invisible
And you're the only one that cries.

Blue are the waves
Lapping the shore.
It's such beautiful scenery,
That no one can ignore.

Blue is the sky,
Blue is the sea.
Such emotions this colour has
That no one can see.

**Jack Denny (12)**
**Cliff Park High School, Gorleston**

# David Blaine

He looks like a rat
He always tries to die,
His voice sounds stoned,
But no one seems to mind.

He currently lives in a box,
Above the River Thames,
Whilst being under attack
By shining laser pens.

It must be very hard,
With no food for six weeks
And without a proper toilet
The place would surely reek.

But he volunteered to go there
And he's been there for five weeks now,
But after a while
It just gets boring.

**Sam Bernthal  (13)**
**Cliff Park High School, Gorleston**

# Red

Red is
flowers, sunrise and more
Red
could also be blood and gore
Red is
smiling and happiness too
Red could be blood or it could
mean love, but one thing is sure
that red could mean anything
Red
depressed, horrible pain
Red
love, peace and fun
Red equals
love, pain, peace, suffering, darkness
happiness, blood - sunrise.
I'm not sure red could mean lots of things,
anything, everything - I am not sure
as red could mean anything.

**Lewis Tyler  (13)**
**Cliff Park High School, Gorleston**

# Wind

It blows the leaves right off the trees,
It blows them all away.
It whistles through the air,
It blows your hats away
But when it stops, there's peace at last,
At least for another day.

In the rain it's annoying,
It blows your umbrellas about.
And if it starts to really blow
It blows them inside out.

It can be fun
For everyone,
So run and grab your kite,
Watch it as it twists whilst in mid-flight.

It blows the leaves right off the trees,
It blows them all away.
It whistles through the air,
It blows your hats away.
But when it stops, there's peace at last,
At least for another day.

**Christopher Smith  (12)**
**Cliff Park High School, Gorleston**

# Fall To Death

Every reflection has a story
Every story has a point
Every point has a vision
Every vision has a dream
Every dream has a worry
Every worry has a victim
Every victim has a fall
Every fall could lead to death.

**Lakhdar Merahi  (13)**
**Cliff Park High School, Gorleston**

# Alone

My life is ruined
A poor child left with nothing.
My mother, a victim,
A victim of a violent partner.
A partner who in the end got the best of her.
Death an awful time in anyone's life -
Simply the hardest thing to cope with
She was so happy,
At her wedding people called them
The perfect couple.
Walking down the aisle, I remember her
As a blushing bride!
Now . . .
I remember her as a vision,
A wreck upon the seabed
Now I am a lonely child
Desperately seeking love.

**Cloe Peters (14)**
**Cliff Park High School, Gorleston**

# Settle For Second Best

My life was so bleak
I would start to sing songs
Someone else's is better
Which means that mine's wrong
My life I would defend
As people invaded
A hand on my cheek
As the reflection faded
I felt so sick
My face is grotesque
Coming to terms that I'm second best.

**Peter Armfield (14)**
**Cliff Park High School, Gorleston**

# Star

I saw a star floating
Then it started to fall,
It had a mission
To wreck my life
And then it was all over.

**Duncan Boyne (12)**
**Cliff Park High School, Gorleston**

# I'm Hungry

Desperately seeking food
need animals to eat.

Found perfect victim,
lying in the sun.
My mission: the kill.

Mmm! That was scrumptious.
Wish I had another!

**Saskia Cook  (12)**
**Cliff Park High School, Gorleston**

# War

It was ruined
death you could call it
it was society that
killed it

Like a plague, it
infected people
killing thousands
it wrecked lives

It's all to do
with two people
who made it
their mission

For them to
disarm Iraq
in that they
killed innocent
people - children
in all, that's why
it should stop!

**Adam Frosdick  (12)**
**Cliff Park High School, Gorleston**

# Food, It Simply Ruined My Diet!

Simply cook for two minutes,
It simply ruined my healthy *diet!*
A perfect two minute meal like
Bangers and mash or something
Like that.
It simply ruined my bloody diet.
I worry about my fat,
Majestic, huge, belly-bursting,
Chubbawabba, stomach.
I think it might *pop!*
*Aaahhh!*
I think it's popped -
That's what I call *bangers!*

**Adam Fairhead  (13)**
**Cliff Park High School, Gorleston**

# Christmas

Rushing down the stairs,
Better hurry up,
Got to get your shoes on
Before Christmas is up.

Scrumptious puddings,
Delicious roasts
And a star for the host.

Christmas trees
Classic Claus
So don't pause

Flashing lights from house to house
The trees glow in the moonlight
So don't catch the next flight
Stay and enjoy Christmas.

Christmas is great
Christmas is good
So come back next year
And have something cooked.

**Samantha Bishop (12)**
**Cliff Park High School, Gorleston**

# Zany

I am me and you are you
I am free and so are you
You are alive, I am dead
But maybe, I've gone off my head!

I am in Heaven
You are on Earth.
You have waves
That you can surf.

I am strange,
As you've guessed!
And you have passed
The strangest test.

**Chloe Simmons (13)**
**Cliff Park High School, Gorleston**

# Dad

Why Dad -
What have you done?
We used to have fun.
Is it my fault you and Mum argue?

I hope you know that you've broken my heart,
I'm missing you Dad, it's tearing me apart.

Where have you gone, I need to see you?
Please come home
But Dad, what have you done?

Just remember, I will always love you
No matter what happens.

**Jordan Lee  (14)**
**Cliff Park High School, Gorleston**

# When Pumbaa Lost Timon!

Timon and Pumbaa went to bed
Pumbaa rolled over and Timon was *dead!*

Pumbaa went to Timon's funeral
He cried so much, he could have
filled a swimming pool!

He went away. Came back today
with a pet turtle, named Ray.

**Simone Garland (13)**
**Cliff Park High School, Gorleston**

# You!

It was the most brightest star you'd ever seen
It was the most delicious food you'd ever eaten
It was the loveliest animal you'd ever touched
It was the most peaceful sound you'd ever heard
You were the most beautiful thing I'd ever seen.

**Keomi Farnsworth  (12)**
**Cliff Park High School, Gorleston**

# Newcastle Are The Best

N ewcastle are the best
E very body knows it.
W onderful players
C reating goals is their game
A nd their colours are black and white,
S hearer is
T heir best player
L ong balls always go to him
E very other player is not as good.
                    Newcastle are the best!

**Connel Hooley  (13)**
**Cliff Park High School, Gorleston**

# The Question I Ask

Why do I look back upon the past?
Why do I look towards the stars to look
and see if you're watching over me?

The question I ask is, 'Would it be different
if you were here to see me grow up?
To see me laugh and to hold me when I cry?'
What would it be like if you were still here?
Would we be happy?
Would we be sad?
Would we be wealthy or would we be poor?'

I think about you all the time,
I wish you were here, so I could hear you laugh
and see you smile.

If only you didn't speed, this wouldn't have happened
and there would be *no sorrow!*

**Luke Prettyman  (15)**
**Cliff Park High School, Gorleston**

# Spontaneously Weird

S imply
P erfectly
O mnipotently
N astily
T otally
A bnormally
N ervous
E xtremely
O r
U nanimously
S illy
L ike
Y aks

W earing
E arrings
I n
R ed
D ominoes/Doritos/delicious deli/delirious dolphins
     and dilapidated dodos
              That's me!

**Adam Cairney (13)**
**Cliff Park High School, Gorleston**

# Katie's Feelings

Frustration
Ears fuming
Gritting teeth
Bloodshot eyes
Pulling hair.

Frustration
Ears fuming
Teeth gritting
Eyes glaring
Hair pulling.

Confusing
Room sharing
Girl confusing
Sharing everything
She's frowning

Fuming!

**Phillippa Pearson (12)**
**Greenfield School Community & Art College, Newton Aycliffe**

# Anger

Heart pounding
Losing temper
Stressed - body squeezing

Fist clenching
Red face
Head banging
Teeth grinding

I'm bored
Eyes dropping
I'm slouched on the couch
Nothing to do
I'm switched off - brain dead

How long will I wait?
I'm bored!

Excitement
I'm excited
Butterflies in my tummy
When am I going to get on?

Time for me
I'm upside down
I feel great

Time to get off
I don't want to
Can I go on again?

**Abbie Sowerby  (11)**
**Greenfield School Community & Art College, Newton Aycliffe**

# The Easter Bunny

What is that?
Is it a bird?
A cloud?
Or a tree?
I don't know,
I whipped on my coat and ran outside
I was shocked to find a golden egg.

Had the world ended without me?
I thought the Easter bunny didn't exist,
When out popped a grey rabbit
Hopping merrily down the road.

**Emma Peart (11)**
**Greenfield School Community & Art College, Newton Aycliffe**

# I Wish I Could Paint . . .

I wish I could paint . . .
a rainbow in the sky.
Trees blowing in the wind,
a summer day in winter.

I wish I could paint . . .
a heart, ticking by like a train.
A house under the crispy winter white snow
and sweets dancing for you and me.

I wish I could paint . . .
a teapot that has to be cracked but is
somehow alright.
A pencil case holding my belongings.
Lights going on and off.

I wish I could paint . . .
feelings, feelings of happiness and
sadness towards you and me.

I wish I could paint!

**Charlotte Howells (11)**
**Greenfield School Community & Art College, Newton Aycliffe**

# My Hates And My Likes

I like to go to the pictures with her
I like to have fun with her
Megan
I like her.

I don't like to hear about it
I don't like to talk about it
Wars
I hate that stuff.

I have to put up with it
I have to listen to it
School
I like that stuff.

I don't like to clean them
I don't like to feed them
Pets
I hate them.

I like to chase them
I like to have fun with them
Boys
I like them.

I'm not interested in it
I don't have fun with it
Science work
I hate it!

I like to be educated by it
I like to enjoy it
English
I like that stuff.

I don't like to dry with them
I don't like to touch them
Tea towels
I hate them!

**Natasha Griffin (12)**
**Greenfield School Community & Art College, Newton Aycliffe**

# My Hates And Likes

They go shopping together
They go to the cinema together
Friends
I like them

Toilets are used for it
School has lots of it
Sick
I hate that stuff

Beaches have lots of it
Fish live in it
Water
I like that stuff

People walk into them
We can open them
Doors
I hate those things

It comes in winter
And it's really special
Christmas
I like that season

It comes all year
And it really wets us
Rain
I hate that stuff

They love me
They spoil me
Family
I love them.

**Megan Davies-Brown   (11)**
**Greenfield School Community & Art College, Newton Aycliffe**

# My Poem

They stand around in checked trousers
With long metal sticks
Golf
I hate that game.

They run around on a pitch
Goal! one-nil
Football
I like that game.

They run around in their cage
With long pink tails
Rats
I hate those things.

They run along the floor
And they have really sharp claws
Cats
I like those animals.

**Matthew Linsley (11)**
**Greenfield School Community & Art College, Newton Aycliffe**

# Tormention

The sun falls after a day
As man sets out to sea
One, two, three, four, five
Times the boat goes *tap, tap*
*Crack!*

Silence as the boat surrenders
To the hungry sea,
The sea speaks to the man
'Thou are not worthy of the sea!'
The man cries as he plummets
To the cold, dark, seabed.

Then a rush of water
He flies to the sky
And wakes upon
An island shore
As he stares at the sea
A tear falls
As he realises he is cursed
With a life of torment.

**Martin Clarke (12)**
**Greenfield School Community & Art College, Newton Aycliffe**

# My Secret Box

Encrusted with diamonds, rubies and sapphires
the box sat gracefully, the glisten of the decor produced a
sparkle in my eyes like that of a clear, blue sky surrounding
a tropical paradise.

I opened the box carefully, my heart beating tenderly
as the beautiful sound emerged - filling the air with warmth and joy
Over and over, the tune played, my mind began to spin,
past memories, experiences, feelings and emotions
swirled in my mind, making me feel warm inside.

The box represented my life. I remembered the very day
I was given the fascinating object and also remembered
everything about my whole life, since that day.

Now my secret box lies untouched by
nobody other than the familiar hands of its loving owner.
But the thing that means the most, is that those familiar
hands belong to me.

**Benita MacDonald (11)**
**Greenfield School Community & Art College, Newton Aycliffe**

# Mommy

'Mommy, Jhonny brought a gun to school today,
he said that he wanted to play.
But Mommy, Jhonny shot the gun,
I heard a scream and began to run.
I'm sorry Mommy, I was too late,
the bullet hit me. Oh no! I'm late!
Please tell my date that I'm sorry,
tell him I loved him, it wasn't just
a crush, and that I'll remember to
wait for him, on hand and foot.

Don't be too long, I'll be sad.
Oh and don't forget to tell Dad I'm
so sorry I couldn't make it in time
for his show.

Please don't be mad, I was dying
in this place, wishing for his debate.
I'm slipping away now, waiting to go,
the angels are here, calling for me . . .'

'Ellie, it's time to leave, don't be scared . . .'

'Remember to tell my friends and family too
I love them so much. Please love me too
but most of all Mommy, I love you.

Please don't forget me in eternity, I certainly
won't you! Remember to keep my room the same.
Don't cry for me I'm too ashamed that I didn't
get away in time.

I should have thought, but I was out of time.
I guess it's just my fate to go so early and
not be late!
I'm sorry Mommy, now I have to go, I'll see you
soon, don't forget to tell everyone too.
I know I can trust you.'

**Gemma Doonan  (11)**
**Greenfield School Community & Art College, Newton Aycliffe**

# Friendship

Friendship is a barrier
surrounding every special soul
thicker than steel.
Friendship is like a twisting river
never knowing where it will go.
Friendship cuts out loneliness and sorrow.
Something quite invisible
but stronger than anything we know.
Chase and destroy our grief
but create our joy.
Never fails, it still grows stronger,
strong until you die.
Friendship is a gentle hand, blessing
every soul from above.

**Vicky Ramsden (12)**
**Hurworth School, Maths & Computing College, Darlington**

# Why?

I wonder why the sky is blue
I wonder why the sea is too.
I wonder why when birds can fly,
I can't, however hard I try.

I wonder if wool comes from sheep
I wonder why I fall asleep
I wonder why the stars are bright
If only I could shine at night

I wonder why my eyes are brown
Or why the Queen wears a crown.
I wonder why the wind can blow
The problem is I'll never know!

**Sophie Miller (11)**
**Hurworth School, Maths & Computing College, Darlington**

# The Sea

Like a great sea monster
It screams and howls
Booming and lowering over
Innocent ships which cower before it.
The sea splashes and swirls,
Dangerously throwing itself about,
But just as dawn breaks, look out to sea.
So innocent, as if nothing happened
So calm, hardly a disturbance across
The water's surface.
As if it's mesmerised and not sure what to do next,
But we know the truth.

**Hannah Barron (11)**
**Hurworth School, Maths & Computing College, Darlington**

# Nature Is A Wonderful Thing

Trees blowing in the wind,
With leaves that fall like feathers,
Blowing branches in the wind,
Nature is a wonderful thing.

Rabbits hopping round and round,
With baby bunnies, they are found
Digging burrows in the wind,
Nature is a wonderful thing.

Birds, flying round and round,
Flying for food, round and down.
*Snap!* They've got a worm,
Nature is a wonderful thing.

Polar bears with furry coats,
Looking like Eskimos as they roam.
Roaming for a tasty seal
Nature is a wonderful thing.

**Hannah Robinson  (11)**
**Hurworth School, Maths & Computing College, Darlington**

# The Cajak

In the night, it roams the hills,
Striking out at lonely mills,
It takes food and runs away
Never seen during the day.

For it's the mighty Cajak
With a score of horns on its back,
Feet, three metres square;
A forked tongue and purple hair.

Many men have tried to tame it,
Many men have failed and blamed it!
For every famine and disease,
It brings the humans to their knees.

For it's the mighty Cajak
With a score of horns on its back,
Feet, three metres square;
A forked tongue and purple hair.

It slavers like a rabid beast,
Upon raw meat it does feast.
Yet it resembles swirling mists,
I wonder if it really exists?

A creature of myth and folklore
Is it alive?
Or is it hunting children for evermore?

**Nick Stockport (11)**
**Hurworth School, Maths & Computing College, Darlington**

# Trevor The Terrier

Trevor the Terrier
nothing to eat
shaking and shivering
alone on the street.

Rampaging dustbins,
hiding from fear,
wishing and hoping
that some help was near.

He used to have a family,
but they didn't care,
although Trevor had feelings,
they weren't aware.

No more than a punchbag
to release day to day stress,
but when they were peaceful
he still was no less.

He was an outcast,
as if he was not there,
but he doesn't deserve this,
it just isn't fair.

Forgotten, ignored,
no answers to desperate cries,
not loved, not walked
but the family told lies.

Trevor took his last kick
against the kitchen wall,
and all his fragile bones were shattered,
as he took his final fall.

**Laura Crawford (11)**
**Hurworth School, Maths & Computing College, Darlington**

# The Sun

The sun relaxes way up high,
shining brightly in the sky,
it bathes silently in a basking yellow,
giving off a glitter glow.

This great ball of fire shoots its light
blasting, heating everything in sight,
but sometimes it gets pushed away,
taken over by weather, cold and grey.

Soon he comes back and hip hip hooray!
Children cheer and go out to play.
The clouds dance around their king
whilst the sun smiles at everything.

**Juliette Clewlow  (11)**
**Hurworth School, Maths & Computing College, Darlington**

# The Night

The night closes on you like a shining door
It's as silent as a tiger waiting to pounce
It's as black as a bucket of fresh coal
With diamonds scattered amongst it
The night grabs at a walker, like a rabid dog, whilst
The moon laughs and stares down at everyone and everything.

It engulfs the sky
Like ink being spilled over a fresh roll of parchment
The night is home to many creatures
A goblin stalks a rabbit with its audience of stars
All watching and waiting for the moment
When the goblin strikes.

The moon and the stars are always in fear
Of the light of the sun and
Of the night leaving them behind
But they never stray off their course
Their task is clear and their duty is fulfilled
They rest now and let the sun move on.

**Christopher Smith (11)**
**Hurworth School, Maths & Computing College, Darlington**

# Sunny Day

Sun shining down
Everyone's around
Rays gently
Shining on
Everyone's in the sun.

Crowded streets
Deckchairs out
Children playing.
All about.

Beautiful sunrays
Beaming down
Beaming on the small town
Setting gently down today
Till another day.

**Laura Ridley  (11)**
**Hurworth School, Maths & Computing College, Darlington**

# My Shadow

It's following me,
Everywhere I go, it's there! Watching me.
It won't go away. It won't leave.

'Leave me alone!' I cried as my voice
echoed through the hall.
'Let me be!'
There was no reply.

Then I saw it, *the thing* that had been
following me.
A misty shadow, moving closer, closer
It spoke -
'I won't leave you alone,' said the voice.
'Not yet!'

'Why?' I said, falling to the ground.
'Because I can't!' the voice was harsh
like a nail scratching down a blackboard.
'Why not?'
'Because, I'm attached to you,
I'm your shadow!'

**Sabrina Baker (11)**
**Hurworth School, Maths & Computing College, Darlington**

# Bob

There once was a man called Bob
Who lived in a place called Slob
He climbed up a tree
But he couldn't see
And he fell down and hit his gob!

The next day he went to his grans
Who had bought fourteen fans
It was very hot
And she had one big spot
So she popped it with two small pans.

Bob then came across a flabagoose
Who looks sort of like a moose
He then found out
It had a spout
For sucking up lots of orange juice.

On his journey he found a mouse
Crossing in front of a very large house
He just avoided
Knocking him over
In his brand new, spanking Rover.

At the end of the day Bob went to his chateau
But found out it had turned into a gateau!
There was the moose
Shouting abuse
Which serves you right, you big fatto!

**Adam Walton  (11)**
**Hurworth School, Maths & Computing College, Darlington**

# In My Land

In my land, trees are like chocolate
Grass is like candyfloss
And flowers are like soft, chewy sweets.

In my land, butterflies never die,
Lions are tame
And dogs are safe from harm.

In my land, stories never end,
Bedtime is exciting
And mornings are full of life.

In my land, war doesn't hurt,
People are kind
And strangers are welcome.

In my land, Heaven is wonderful,
Wishes come true
And the world is as peaceful as a sleeping mouse.

**Elizabeth Doubleday  (11)**
**Hurworth School, Maths & Computing College, Darlington**

# Behind The Plug

The monster that lives behind the plug,
When it drains you can hear it glug!
It roars and roars until it's dry,
I really hate it cos it makes me cry.

I told my mum but she don't care,
To tell the truth I think it's a bear,
I told my friend but she didn't believe me,
Until she came round to tea.

It howled and growled louder than ever,
I bet it didn't feel clever,
My mum came rushing in, in a bit of a panic,
She looked like a ghost who had drunk
Too much, gin and tonic.

She told us the whole of the story,
That he wasn't a monster and was called Rory,
From that day on, I was never scared
When he growled, I said, 'I don't care!'

**Tom Dell (11)**
**Hurworth School, Maths & Computing College, Darlington**

# The Sky

The clouds in the sky, fluffy like cotton wool,
Suddenly change, became grey and dull.

Sometimes the sky is blue and bright,
Sun shining, yellow like daffodils,
Such a beautiful sight.

But the wind changes, there's a nip in the air,
Soon snow starts to fall and it's too cold to bear.

The sky is forever changing,
We can't always predict what
The weather will be.
But whatever happens to the sky
It's always an interesting sight, to see.

**Natalie Lawson  (11)**
**Hurworth School, Maths & Computing College, Darlington**

# Toon Army

Here we go, we're on our way
Toon Army are here to stay
Hear us come
Hear us go
Watch us shout
Here we go!

Salano kicked the ball
It went higher and higher.
The ball didn't pass
That Kieran Dyer.
Alan Shearer, what a goal scored
When the ball went in the net
The whole crowd roared!

Toon Army are in the match
David Seaman, has shaved his tash!
Man City lost, they'll soon regret
We are the Toon Army
The best team yet.

**Jack Pedleham (11)**
**Hurworth School, Maths & Computing College, Darlington**

# The Jungle

Early in the morning, down in the jungle,
The snakes start to slither around the bamboo trees,
The elephant's awake from their long night's sleep.
All the animals come down to the watering hole,
For their morning drink,
The baby tigers start to play
While their dads go out hunting.

He sees a deer,
He crouches down while watching the
Deer comes towards him.
He pounces,
The deer jumps like a Jack-in-the-box and dashes off.
The tiger springs to life and dashes after it,
But it gets away, this time!

**Charlotte Harker  (11)**
**Hurworth School, Maths & Computing College, Darlington**

# The Bear Cub's Mother

She sleeps all day, she sleeps all night,
Under frosty snows,
She hibernates when it's light,
And when howling winds do blow.

The scent of spring
Comes drifting in
To her hollow, underground hole.
She wakes with a roar,
And shouts, 'I want to sleep more!'

She stomps out, without a doubt,
To catch some trout,
For her hungry cubs,
(Because at the moment
The hunters are in the pubs).

She growls like a car
And she travels so far,
For the catch of the day,
Like any mother would.

**Laura Carter  (11)**
**Hurworth School, Maths & Computing College, Darlington**

# The Storm

Waves crashed and bashed against the deck,
Sea was like a boiling cauldron,
Wind howling
Sails flapping.

As the night went on the
Sea calmed and those
That were sleeping were unharmed.

**Emily Bell (12)**
**Hurworth School, Maths & Computing College, Darlington**

# The Lion

He waits in the golden grass
For the time to come,
Hoping his prey will soon pass.
He sees it miles away,
Prancing, dancing with no fear,
It starts to go the lion's way
It doesn't know its end is near.

The lion swoops like a bird,
Pearly-white teeth become bloodstained
As they sink into the innocent flesh.
Then no sound, nothing is heard,
But the sound of the lion, finishing its meal.

**Laura Mills  (11)**
**Hurworth School, Maths & Computing College, Darlington**

# The Christening

The day of the christening and everybody is preparing,
The parents, the godparents,
The caterers and the people of the church.

Friends and family arriving at the church,
Stained-glass windows fragment the light into rainbow colours.
In the background the organ plays,
As the coming together of old friends happens all around.
The vicar speaks and says the prayer.
Everybody using golden voices to sing the hymns.
The child, centre of the occasion, is anointed;
The child is baptised.
Unknowing the child looks around,
Seeing faces not knowing they are here for him.

The party afterwards people laugh and talk,
The caterers back-breaking work has pleased the guests.
Gifts of many kinds are brought forth for the child;
Unknowing the child looks around.

Young and old talk;
The old talk of how they knew the young,
When they were younger still.
And the young try to imagine the youth the old have left behind.
Time passes and none realise.
We toast the newly anointed child,
We cut the cake in his name;
And now the day has ended and the child lies in his cot,
Unknowing that this day has been for him.

**Joseph Phelps  (11)**
**Northgate High School, Dereham**

# To My Loving Family

We got real close to enemy lines today,
I've seen so much suffering on the way.
People torn from limb to limb,
It happened to my best mate Jim.
I'm not ashamed to say I cried,
He called for his dad as he died.
What a waste of such a young life,
He left behind his pregnant wife.
I'm so scared, this will be my last night,
I'm shivering, not with cold but with fright.
The noise of the guns hurt my ears,
We tell stupid jokes to hide our fears.
How can this war be so full of hate?
I hope it ends soon, before it's too late.
I've seen friends run screaming, flames in their hair,
The smell of burnt flesh hangs in the air.
I heard our bomber planes flying overhead,
I can't be happy, knowing people are dead.
Every time we move forward rank by rank,
We pray we don't come across an enemy tank.
One platoon did and there's no ifs or buts,
All of them were left, just blood and guts.
We came across one, his eyes open wide,
As he tried to push his intestines inside.
He died so slowly so full of pain,
Alone full of fear am I going insane?
This is madness, to kill those you don't know,
But we aim and shoot, or grenades we throw.
Well it's time to move on, is this goodbye?
Is this the end? Am I going to die?
I see people wishing on their luck charms,
I wish I were there in your loving arms.

**Clinton Thompson (15)**
**Northgate High School, Dereham**

# Eternal Memories

What would you do if your whole life
Just collapsed around you one day
And everything that you once knew
Just vanished right away?

It would take all your courage to stop you
From running right away
It would be so hard just to keep sane
In the face of so much pain.

We are worried about terrorists
And what else will go wrong
But what about the children
Whose parents are now gone?

What will these kids do
Whose parents have been stolen away?
Though they will try and forget the hurts
The memories will never fade.

We have to stop the terrorists
From thinking what they do is cool
We all must aim to live in peace
For our and our children's futures too.

**Bethany Farrow  (12)**
**Northgate High School, Dereham**

# My Family

My dad, he is so tall and strong
He stands so proud and true
My dad, he is so kind and wise
I look up to him no matter what my size

My mum, she is so loving and caring
She is always there for me
My mum is my best friend
I will love her to the end

My brother, he is so annoying
He is a pain, but can be funny
My brother and I always argue and fight
But I love him and I will defend him with all my might

My dog, he is a bundle of fun
He is really cute and cuddly
My dog, he enjoys his walks and eating a bone
He is always there for me when I get home

Last but not least it's me
I am devoted to my family
I will love them all my days
Even when we go our different ways.

**Abigail Roberts  (12)**
**Northgate High School, Dereham**

# The Dragon

There is a land so far away,
It remains undiscovered unto this day.
The land is healthy, broad and green,
The land of the dragon, Scarnameen.

Scarnameen is a dark red dragon,
A scathing, raving, ferocious dragon.
His flaming breath will scorch the land,
The trees, fields, earth and sand.

The people, scared and terrorised,
Sought out a hero to bring its demise.
The monster has ruined our crops of food,
Bring us from the darkness of its foul, fiery mood.

Then from the crowd, a short cry arose,
'I could do the job I suppose.
It is about time for that creature to go,
And all I will need is the foot of a crow.'

The people turned, and saw, and gasped,
And so the hero slowly rasped:
'I may be small, and thin, and tragic,
But I will vanquish the dragon by use of magic.'

And so the day came to arise,
When food was scarce and in short supplies.
The hero set out to find the dragon,
With the foot of a crow, and a small wooden flagon.

He journeyed through mountains and into a dell,
Where he shuffled along then tripped and fell.
The dragon bore down on him, snorted and snapped,
But it didn't realise it had been trapped.

The hero leapt up to his feet and yelled,
The words of pure *magic* so clearly spelled.
*'By wooden cup and foot of crow,*
*I order this dragon to quietly go.'*

And then, as if in the calm of day,
The monster got up and flew quickly away.
It is seen once more in our modern world,
As fumes and pollution, how very absurd!

**Sam Mitchell-Finnigan (12)**
**Northgate High School, Dereham**

# I Am But The Devil's Seed

Take the long, hard road out of Hell and maybe you'll see
The scriptures on my wrists
Take care not to spill your foolish pride
Crack open the jam jar to reveal the pain
I was so lucid like the end impending
The smoke of the burning corpses
And take my hand, to clarity we'll climb . . .
So push my hands through the thorns to crush a rose
And in craving catch my blood
Your hands a nailed cross, anticipation carnates us all
I am but all your deepest fears, your shallowest graves
And in darkness I'll snatch what is rightfully yours
With love, with tears, I'll rip it right out
Your heart a tiny blood clot

Think twice before you open your mouth
I am but devious, mistakable for the Devil they say
Restlessness consumes my fading memories
The grave was all but a fine momento
I am the veiled, I am the darkened
I am the omnipotent nurturing malevolence
Hell was passion but that's long gone
And I am the killer's breed, the demon's seed
A love of the living dead, that's thy
So I'll pity your soul in the rudest manner
And I'll watch as your skin sinks into the crawl
But escape as your plea, plead as you may
Together we'll transcend to the land that I loved
For your time has come to let animosity unwind
Your time has come to be bitten by thy poison

Some say that eternity is hard to grasp
But infinity is far harder to comprehend
Yes I have and no I've not
Christ's crucifixion commercials failed a long time ago
Blaspheme is a phrase, oh my heart bleeds in sacrament
We can all be martyrs - just thrust a crown and you'll see

I have no shame, I have no sorrow
And you'll wait and we'll wait and they'll wait
And buy death by the tarot, the priest, the television
And still I'll sell controversy - oh life is so meaningless

So kiss goodbye to those days of true love and lipstick on linen
And wave hello to my open palms of bloodshed
No god is good enough to save you from my hatred
No god is powerful enough to save you from my rapacious ways
The angel's in the lobby, the folklore down the gutter
So once again I'll spill the pain
And watch as you walk that long, hard road out of Hell
For the Devil is yet to be slaughtered . . .

**Lauren Meecham (13)**
**Northgate High School, Dereham**

# Who Will Be Next?

As I stare up at the night sky,
The edge of the blood-red moon glints cold and hard,
Into the deep darkness I wonder,
How could it bring so much pain and despair?
There are no stars, no hope, no faith,
It all went when death came banging on the door,
Like thunder in a storm,
It made a shiver run tingling down my spine,
As the footsteps of doom,
Pounded even closer,
There were no screams, no shouts for help,
It was so quick, like a knife in the darkness,
Not seen until it's too late,
I cried out, but they had gone.
I was alone in the deep night,
With the spirits of innocence,
I can trust no one, I cannot believe,
It is not fair,
Why? What have we done wrong?
I sit alone and wonder,
If up there they are free,
Form the death, terror and deceit,
That rules here on earth,
I wonder like a lonely soul,
Who will be next?

**Rachel Lawrence (14)**
**Northgate High School, Dereham**

# Poet Laureate Poem - The Snow

I sit watching the snow drift down like confetti,
The wind stirs it up and howls through the land,
A rabbit darts towards its burrow,
A bird struggles to get through the wind.

The trees are dusted in snow and look like ghosts,
The wind makes them sway dangerously,
A robin flies towards a tree with its nest in it,
It gets blown back, but does reach its nest.

The world is now covered in a blanket of snow,
Everything is only visible by its outline as more snow falls,
Darkness is drawing in and I can't see much now,
The wind has calmed and the stars are now out.

Outside is so dark I can hardly see anything,
I can just make out the fence and the trees,
It is so dark I stop looking at the snow,
Instead I turn to watch my fire blaze brightly.

**George Hewson  (13)**
**Northgate High School, Dereham**

# Every Night

Every night I stand and stare,
Just looking through the empty air.
Looking for a single trace,
Of that joyous, fun-filled place.

Every night I wonder where,
Where the people I knew have gone.
How did they get there? Are they returning?
My desire to know this is always burning.

Every night I want to know,
Know where the people I know go,
Want to know why they disappear,
Without a single sorrow or fear.

Every night I wish and wish,
Wishing that they will return,
So I can see their faces again,
So I can run around with them.

Every night I wonder why,
Why the people I know die,
Every night I stand and stare,
Every night I wonder where.

Every night I wish and wish,
Every night I want to know,
Want to know where dead souls go
Every night.

**Daniel Clark (13)**
**Northgate High School, Dereham**

# Birds Of The Wilderness

Birds of the wilderness
Were soaring overhead
Skimming all the treetops
Hovering through our flight.

The breeze rushing through my feathers
Whistling as it goes
I'm eyeing up my food tonight
My mouth pouring as I do.

I wait and wait
For the pounce to come
Gliding downwards so cautiously
That my prey hasn't even noticed he's dinner tonight.

I smell danger
Humans are down below
I see blood
And something long and shiny.

I pause, hovering in mid-air
A plane comes over low and I'm spotted
Where to hide?
I flap faster as he reaches for the gun
As instant as a fox, he pulls the trigger
I shiver in pain, my thoughts whirling, I'm dead.

**Josephine Ogbourne  (13)**
**Northgate High School, Dereham**

# Memory

I worked so hard
Farming the land,
Soon I had two sons
To give me a hand.

Time went by
Oh so fast,
The 1930's depression
Was soon in the past.

Another war,
Another fight,
Bombs were falling
Day and night.

My father and mother,
Brother and his son,
Were lost forever
When the fighting was done.

My life was half over
When a new queen was crowned,
Watching the coronation
With grandchildren around.

Stories I told them
While sitting by the fire,
I'm sure they thought
I was a liar!

Stop all your doctors,
Stop staring at me,
A grumpy old man,
Is that what you see?

If you had seen
All that's happened in my life,
The birth of my children,
The death of my wife.

The year was 1900
When I gave my first cry,
So long ago,
Now I'm ready to die.

But my head's full of memories,
Some good, some bad,
Remembering the Titanic,
That makes me so sad.

Along came the war,
My dad had to go,
The time he was gone,
It went so slow.

Then it was my turn,
When I came of age,
Each terrifying moment
Written on my diary page.

At last I was home,
And married my sweetheart,
The journey was so bumpy
On that rickety hay cart.

How fashions did change,
Mini skirts then flares,
Flower power and Afros,
Youths without care.

Those wonderful holidays,
Miles of golden sand,
Warm seas and pebbles,
My, it was grand.

So stop all you doctors,
Stop staring at me,
I've seen more than you have,
So go get my tea.

**Jake Hardiment (13)**
**Northgate High School, Dereham**

# What I See Through My Window

The soft mist floats through the open window,
The smell of a fresh day wafts about,
Mingled in is the scent of newly baked bread,
Daylight breaks through the window lighting all near.

Twitter go the birds hopping from bud to bud on each tree,
New is the spring, lacy dew on the ground, flowering,
Flowering the daffodils, nodding in the sun,
A sweet perfume of fresh flowers came through the window.

Tulips and bluebells poking their heads out of the churned soil,
Facing the fiery sun, swaying in the breeze, smiling,
Smiling to the new day, which is dawning,
The beauty of the world shone through the window.

Hear, the church bells toll, ringing in the early morn,
Ringing over the valley, from in the lowly church,
Daisies in the meadow, cow bells ring in the pasture,
Peace and tranquillity floated through the open window.

Turn, turn again and see the concrete and the brick,
Hear the endless roar of cars, buses and taxis,
Business parks, hotels, shops, flats and malls take over the green
                                  and turn it to a boring grey,
I shut my window to the heavy smoke and fumes and turn my back
                                  on the endless sea of concrete.

**Rachel French (12)**
**Northgate High School, Dereham**

# War

It's been going on for years,
Before I even existed.
The pain, the hurt and killing about,
Yet it never stops, why?

Nobody cares, they have no respect,
Why treat people differently?
They are just like me or you,
Yet it never stops, why?

It shouldn't matter,
What religion, what colour.
We are all the same,
Yet it never stops, why?

My dad went to war,
Fighting for his beliefs,
He stood up for his rights,
It stopped for him, why?

**Nicki Colville (13)**
**Northgate High School, Dereham**

# In The Future

As she stands there waiting and waiting, her hand clasped tightly
to her support.
Her back is bent double as her frail body leans against her trolley.
Shopping, clothes, food and gifts overflow from the old, blue,
battered bag.
Groceries and possessions wearing and pulling her down.

As my eye line travels up towards her face.
Her small brown eyes sunk back in her head stare back.
A sweet smile appears with her lips folded back into her mouth
and rimmed with stubly facial hairs.
Framing her face is a thin, grey mop of hair.
It's pulled back into a clasp and gathered under a white woolly hat.
Some wispy strands of hair dangle in front of her face
as they move and blow in the wind.

Wrinkles map out her face like roads all connecting
and interlinking with each other.
Down and down everything falls.
Her skin hangs closer to the ground from her deformed
and brittle skeleton.
A dress, lightly patterned with a chequered embroidery, slightly faded
and threadbare is left to blow in the wind.
It is smothered by a crocheted cardigan made from yards and yards
of thick, warm wool.
Dull, green buttons line her torso, fastening her tea-stained
cardi together.
Buttons, zips and poppers surround her arms as her cuffs
are neatly folded away off her hands.
Tucked into this mass of materials is a delicate purple scarf.
It is encasing her head in a loop which traps everything in one position.
Beneath all of this lies her head,
Barely reaching the surface to breathe before it is sucked under
by her suffocating clothes.

As the bus rolls up, she is confused and dazzled by the simple task
of finding some money from her purse.
She is blown back by a mass of bustling strangers as she steps
onto the bus platform.
Deep inside she tuts at 'the youth of today'.
Soon she's off and she toddles home.

She slowly sits down in an armchair,
Puts on her slippers, as her stockings fall and crease round her ankles.
She's alone once more.
As a wireless blares into her two deaf ears,
Pills and throat sweets are taken,
Fears of her safety grow inside.

In bed, beneath her sheets and blankets, her eyelids close.
She can rest in peace, locked away from the world.
Can't she?
Oh what will I do, how will I manage when she is me?

**Madeleine Moore (13)**
**Northgate High School, Dereham**

# The Greatest Ship Ever Built

They thought it so mighty,
So strong;
Never to sink,
They were wrong.
Something unexpected happened,
Something they didn't think of.
It was a terrible tragedy,
Thank God there were survivors to tell the story;
Of the greatest ship
Ever to be built.
If the iceberg was not there,
Would there have been a chance
For them all to survive?
We will never know.
If the thousands of lost lives,
Would have come home.
To tell the story of the best
And most magical voyage of their lives.
To have made the film again,
To have a happy ending.
With tears of happiness in our eyes.
Not sorrow.

**Kerry Cordell (13)**
**Northgate High School, Dereham**

# Chaos

Chaos is the root of all things dark
It looks at you with a grin of a shark
Black fingers are a sure sign
That people with them are not fine
Goths, some call them, they relish the name
They want to show they're not the same
Darkness has them in its cool grip
They've jumped overboard on purity's ship
Chaos seduces all it can
God forever has it on ban.

**Michael Robson (14)**
**St Leonard's RC Comprehensive School, Durham**

# Suicide

I was on the edge,
I had to hide,
I was on the brink of suicide,
I came back,
I found my place, my time, my pride,
No longer do I have to hide,
No longer I feel suicide.

**Matthew James Turnbull  (15)**
**St Leonard's RC Comprehensive School, Durham**

# The Night Of The Crowd

As the crowd begins to appear,
I know it's near,
The roar of the people,
I will start to hear,
As the curtains come up,
I come to a stop,
I can't hear myself,
My ears are going to pop,
The sound of the crowd,
Makes me come alive,
As the night comes to a draw,
The crowd, they want more,
The curtains go down,
As I wave my farewell,
I think to myself,
This night went well.

**Katie McElroy (15)**
**St Leonard's RC Comprehensive School, Durham**

# Cats And Dogs

C rouching hidden like a tiger,
A crobatic on the grass,
T he night-time falls, their eyes are watching, watching,
S itting ready, ready to jump, play and run.

*And*

D rooling over last night's dinner,
O nce again they're licking, licking,
G rowling at the next-door neighbours,
S weet puppy eyes staring at the snacks and biscuits.

**Amy Spence (14)**
**St Leonard's RC Comprehensive School, Durham**

# Goodbye Stranger

You were just here,
But now you're gone,
Never so much have I missed anyone,
You were great and I loved you so,
But why on earth did you have to go?
I want to tell you so many things,
I sit by the phone and hope it rings,
But it's no good, you're not coming back,
Where are you at?
At least tell me that,
Tell me when you are coming home,
Today, tomorrow, I'll be by the phone.

**Sarah Clough  (14)**
**St Leonard's RC Comprehensive School, Durham**

# The North East Of England

The north east of England is the place to be
We've got McDonald's, Burger King and KFC
The north east of England is the place to go
We've got MVC, City Sports and Kascada Bowl
The north east of England is the place to stay
Football and rugby is what we like to play
All in all I've got to say
The north east of England is the perfect place for a holiday.

**Robert Miles (14)**
**St Leonard's RC Comprehensive School, Durham**

# The Iron Maiden

The Iron Maiden standing tall
The Iron Maiden cold and hard
The Iron Maiden with no sound at all
The Iron Maiden fist of weight
The Iron Maiden lifeless as a rock

I toss him a guitar!

The Iron Maiden still standing tall
But
The Iron Maiden warm and soft
The Iron Maiden with the sound of cords
The Iron Maiden fingers of speed
The Iron Maiden jumping off the floor
The Iron Maiden is now ready to *rock*.

**Ben Jones (14)**
**St Leonard's RC Comprehensive School, Durham**

# The Place That I Live

Newcastle and Durham
Rivers flow through freely in both
Mines go miles under the ground
Twisting and turning for eternity
The Angel of the North
A pile of rust with a meaning
An angel protector maybe?
Two rivers flow to the sea
Bridges taking us over the Tyne and Wear
Two communities able to communicate by bridges
The home I live in
Filled with love and furniture
The north east has a lot of history
This is the place that I live.

**Maria Smith  (15)**
**St Leonard's RC Comprehensive School, Durham**

# All About A Mouse

Spheres brown
Bristles furry
Eyes watching
Short claws and a very long tail
Like a snake.

**Steven Wright (13)**
**Sheringham Woodfields (Special) School, Sheringham**

# Worm

Black mud
Brown, lumpy string
Thin and long
She slowly slithers.

**Andrew Easton (11)**
**Sheringham Woodfields (Special) School, Sheringham**

# Caterpillar

Spiked moustache
Tiny veins
Yellow circles and green pointed end
It crawls and trails.

**Frank Butt (13)**
**Sheringham Woodfields (Special) School, Sheringham**

# Mole

Tunnelling claws
Hairy, soft
Pink cones, slimy
Eyes blind.

**Danny Bridges  (13)**
**Sheringham Woodfields (Special) School, Sheringham**